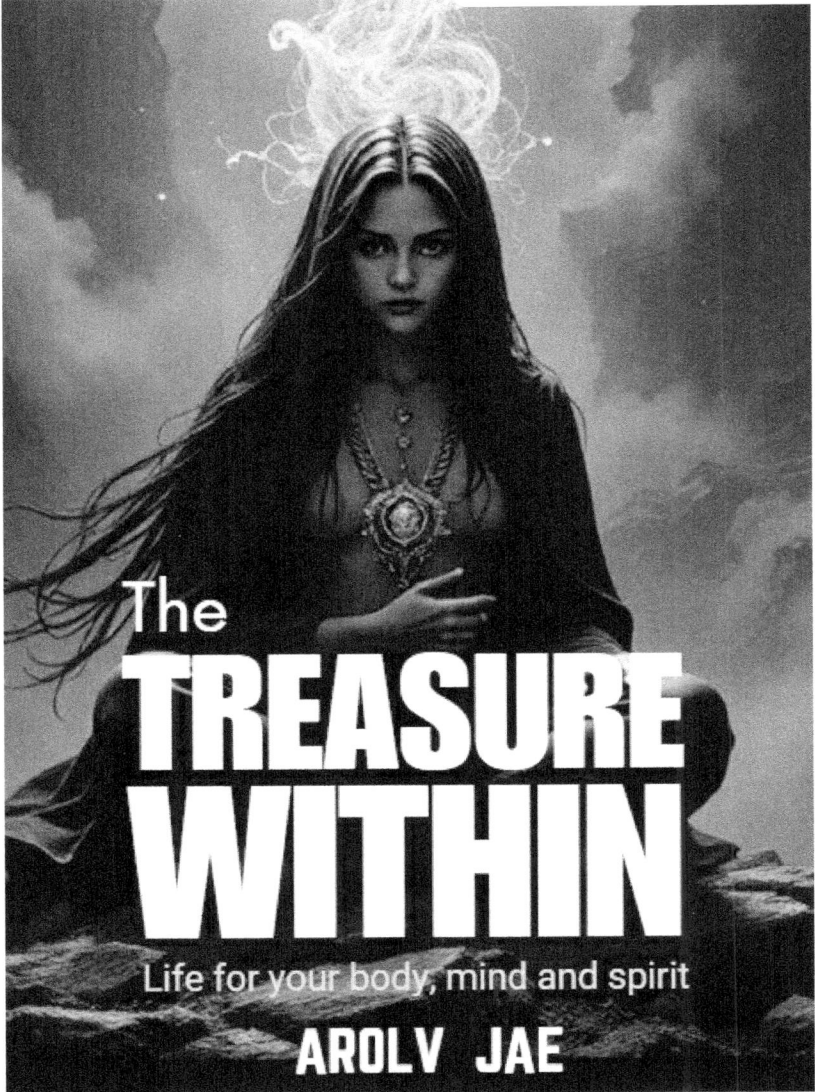

# The
# TREASURE
# WITHIN

## Life for your body, mind and spirit

### AROLV JAE

**ISBN** 9798308232049

# CONTENTS

## PART **THREE** – SOUL, **THE TRUE DIVINE SELF**

## PART **FOUR** – SEXUAL ENERGY – CONTINENCE

# PART FIVE – A LITTLE BIT OF THIS & A LITTLE BIT OF THAT

## AUTHOR'S NOTE

As an individual, I have enough thoughts to write a whole book based on personal experiences. My intention is to lead you within, in remembering who, what you are and what you are capable of. You are already a limitless being. But to bring remembrance of that, it is important to read multiple books and research beyond book reading. Reading only my thoughts is like dipping your feet in a pond. In this book I will try to mention as many books as possible, sometimes I will mention passages and/or excerpts more than once from the same source (books, websites, or YouTube etc.).

By being exposed to other sources besides my own, you will not just dip your feet, but you will dive in an ocean of knowledge, *innerstanding and wisdom. And when/if you decide to look into those sources, then you will dive even deeper since those sources mention many other sources for the readers/listeners. When I read other author's books, as soon as I see another author's book mentioned in the book, I immediately go on Amazon and look the book up. I don't care about reviews (even though sometimes I check on them), I take my chances.

When you take your chances you discover more, but if you don't get a book or any products because a reviewer didn't like it, then you are losing on information. The reviewer that didn't like it, expressed his/her opinion based on his/her level of innerstanding themselves. If you decide to act in life based on what others think about life, then you are simply following that person rather than being your own leader. I won't go on any more about this "reviewing on Amazon" subject, but when/if you decide to get the book, "You Are The One" by Pine G. Land, at the end of Pine's book, there are 2-3 pages talking about reviewing products on Amazon. I loved the way the author of that book thinks. Throughout the book I will mention at least a quote from that book. I just recently began using the word "innerstand" which means to understand from within. I got bombarded (for a good reason) with the word innerstanding from a few books which will be mentioned throughout the chapters of this book.

No matter how true information in this book may seem, no matter how much you resonate with my words, you must not believe anything, you must only know something to be true and not to believe it to be true. We constantly change, every day, whether we realize it or not. Just by reading my train of thought in this book, it is like adding a new (or different amount of) ingredient in the soup (mind). And you know what happens if you add more ingredients or a different amount, the food tastes different. The same applies here. Everything you read/hear here or anywhere else, it gets automatically recorded in your subconscious. Then, eventually, depending on the circumstances in your life and how determined you are with your choices, you will decide to use a specific combination of thoughts which derives from knowledge you have acquired from books, social media or talks with friends, siblings or strangers.

**1-** "Tell me who you hang around with and I'll tell you who you are".

**2-** "Tell me what book you read, what social media accounts you follow, how you think, or how you act daily and I'll tell you whether you are on the right track or not".

**Number 1** – My parents used to tell me this for a long time when I was growing up. In our society you are surrounded by all kinds of people; people who want you to be happy and those who don't. Without you realizing, a little at a time when you hang out with people of low vibration, you will be sucked into low vibrational field patterns, and you may become like them. Better to be alone and to listen to your inner voice rather than hanging around with low vibrational people just because you want to be validated, approved or any other reasons that you may think you need to hang around with. You can care and love someone without having to be near them. In this case, I mean for example, a cousin or a friend or a sibling that doesn't live in the same house with you.

A lot of people aggravate each other, but if you keep your distance, there is a chance that your mental and emotional health will improve. If you are cooking something in high heat and you cover the pot, after a while the liquid/food may spill. For that to not happen, you must take off the lid from the pot or lower the heat. In the case of interaction between people, we must take a deep breath, think for ourselves, take some time away from the heat (interacting with people of a different vibe).

**Number 2** - The whole universe exists within yourself. Anything external is a projection from within. For example, the internet is a projection of all of us on a collective level. Even if it wasn't you that created the internet, those who created it, had to create it based on our collective request. The more people struggle in life, the more our souls yearn for freedom. Guess what the internet is; it is freedom. In the recent decade there have been more immigrants than ever. It is easy to travel with airplanes, or fast boats and other means. Millions of immigrants communicate with their loved ones through social media or different communication apps.

Decades ago, you had to mail a letter to someone, and it could take days to reach the person. Now, with the internet you can not only text, but you can facetime and communicate with people as if you are in front of them. Just like anything else, the internet can be abused. The internet is good but also bad if you search/follow low frequency content or even if you search/watch/listen to good content if you spend all your day online. Life is not for just being online, because there are many beautiful things outside of technological screens.

English is the author's 3rd language, so the content of this book is written as if you are face to face, having a coffee or lunch with the author. The author is not a people pleaser. The author would rather trigger someone (for the purpose of healing and understanding) by speaking his/her mind, rather than being a people pleaser. We cannot grow in comfort. Getting triggered is good, as long as we use the triggering as a catalyst for overall improvement of our physical, mental and spiritual state.

"All the seeking and the searching outside of yourself, will eventually lead you within, but it may take you one year, fifty years or multiple lifetimes; when you search within, all the answers will appear. Go within, that's where the well of knowledge is. Within you resides raw creative divine power. By transmuting this divine power, it turns you into a Superman/ Superwoman. What you feed your body and your mind, will affect your spirit. Use your currency/energy wisely and your whole body will be filled with light". - *Arolv Jae*

# PART ONE
## THE PHYSICAL MARVEL

# B O D Y

"This physical body that you have been carrying all along since birth, is the greatest thing ever gifted to you. You have been living in the most advanced piece of technology ever created. Take care of it, or there will be consequences if you operate through carelessness"
*- Arolv Jae*

Why do we strive to be healthy? Why do we want to live longer? Because we appreciate life. Which means that there is something in us that tells us we do not have to die. Death is the end of life as we know it, but that's just an illusion; death is one side of life, with the other side being the afterlife (the other life). We are too convoluted/magnificent creatures to just pay bills, have children, work and then die. There is much more than a mundane low vibrational existence. Most of us roam the surface of the Earth in an unconscious state, we go here and there, indulge in food, drinks, and sex without seeing what's beyond our narrow field of vision. There is much more to life than wasting our time with politics, sports, gossip, materialistic gadgets etc. The physical vessel is but a temporary shell, housing the spirit (a small part of it, while the rest of the spirit is elsewhere).

We eat to fill our belly, we eat to the point that our senses are numbed down. We have become a very emotional species and overanalyze everything. We do everything to satisfy our 5 senses, except for feeding our soul. We are so overwhelmed with a mundane life that we live in a mental and emotional prison. We forget how to breathe deeply. People's senses are shut down from being over-medicated. The anti-aging solution is found in breathing patterns and not in supplements or any other kind of pills.

Breathe, breathe, breathe slower and deeper. The faster you breathe (with the exception of when you exercise), the shorter your life becomes. When energy channels flow properly in the body, you barely need to sleep anymore. Why do people love to sleep? Why not love being awake? Have you ever heard anyone saying they don't like to sleep, or that they don't enjoy sleeping? With the exceptions when someone had a rough night and couldn't sleep well but that's tied to one of the two reasons. Two reasons why people like to sleep:

**One**-Because of being tired of the daily unhealthy routine and **Two**-Because of the soul wanting to go back to Source where suffering doesn't exist.

Why do you need to sleep, why does the body get tired? We are full of energy by default, but through our choices we suppress much of the energy or we waste it. One major problem is eating three meals a day. Eating many times a day keeps people in the lower three energy centers or chakras. The body requires a significant amount of energy to process and digest the food we eat. And even more if the food is toxic and unhygienic. Fasting is very good in allowing the body to heal itself. One cannot become sick and be healed at the same time, meaning that you cannot heal yourself by eating but by not eating (fasting).

## S2 GROUNDING, MOTHER EARTH'S MEDICINE

We are designed to walk, among many other things. If we walk at least half an hour to an hour per day, it can add years to our life. If we do not walk, the blood doesn't flow regularly, it will concentrate in the liver, it will not absorb clean oxygen. Not enough oxygen will go to the muscles, blood, organs etc. Since we now know beyond doubt that clean oxygen (through diaphragmatic breathing) prolongs life, then by not walking at all or not enough, we set ourselves up for premature aging, and slow death. If you walk barefoot on soil or the grass, it is even better. This way, any energy stagnancy will be transported in the ground/soil and you will receive healing/free flowing radicals/energy from the mother earth.

Walking improves memory, reduces depression, it can cut obesity by half. Even if you are not obese, you must walk. Even if you never get fat, it does not mean that you are healthy. Walking is beneficial to both physical and mental health and it can be done anywhere, it burns calories and simply feels good. Even if it is raining outside, you can walk in the house, it is what I do. If you live in a house that has floors, then go up and down the floors a few times and you will see your heart beating faster, which is good.

The blood and the brain (and the whole body) get oxygenated, but also the heart muscles get exercise. If you suffer from anxiety, just walking regularly, it should help reduce it. If you can (I do not see a reason why not), listen to the music when you practice any kind of exercise. For two reasons, one because music is food for your soul, without music there cannot be a joyous and fulfilling life. And secondly, by listening to the music you are focused mostly on the music instead of analyzing the surroundings.

## S3 HEELS KILL PHYSICAL BODY STRUCTURE

We emit a signal every moment of every day, at all times. The biggest part of that signal is the tension stored inside of us, holding us out of balance. When our feet are placed in such an unnatural position, we compensate in other areas to keep ourselves in balance. But it's not an aligned balance, it's a compensated balance. We have to hold ourselves tight in other areas - our feet, legs, hips, stomach muscles, shoulders, and necks are all compensating for the unnatural angle of our feet. That tension affects the signal we emit - we are no longer our "true" selves, because that tension keeps us unbalanced. I wonder if that is something men realized, because it used to be men who wore high heels. High heels were made for the inverted. Fake men wore them because they were usually too small and fake women wear those nowadays to mimic the feminine curved spine and pelvic tilt.

A successful **podi**atrist (podi in Greek means 'foot') in Canada revealed the majority of his business comes from women who have wreaked havoc on their physiology, joints, tendons, etc, from wearing high heels. Another insane manifestation of the patriarchy is that in the UK they ruled it is legal to discriminate against women in the workplace who don't want to wear high heels and force them to wear them as part of their uniform. Literally forcing them to damage their entire physiology, toes to spine to hips to neck, in order to keep a job, for this absurd beauty standard.

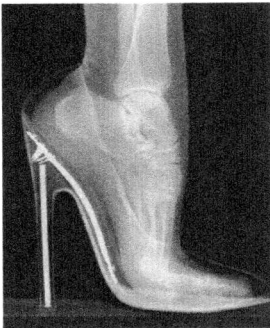

Wearing high heeled shoes causes arthritis and damaged knees. Shoes with high heels are the fashion choice for many women around the world. Study proves without a doubt that wearing high heels over a long period of time can permanently injure the body. The study is from Stanford University in the USA. A team of biomotion researchers did tests on the knees of women when they walked in flat shoes, shoes with 3.8-cm heels and in shoes with 8.9-cm heels. The results send a warning to women who want to wear high heels that they risk permanent damage to their knees. They said high heels put knees in an awkward, bent position that makes them function like aged or damaged joints. This increases the risk of the condition osteoarthritis, which could require surgery.

Britain's Daily Express newspaper reports a recent survey of 1,200 women that shows how popular high heels are. It said 93 per cent of women say they felt sexier and more feminine when they wore heels, 88 per cent said they considered themselves more stylish and 77 per cent said their heels made them feel slimmer.

Many women prefer to ignore health warnings, and even the pain and discomfort of wearing heels, to look and feel good. A British doctor, Tim Allardyce, said he regularly treats women with problems caused by wearing heels. He said: "*The odd angle at which the feet are held in high-heeled shoes increases the downward pressure on the knees by 25 per cent, placing significant stress on the kneecaps.*"

If you need external products (high heels, sexually revealing clothing, make up, fake nails/nail polish, beauty products) to feel sexy, then you don't know that you are already sexy. When you feel sexy and alive according to your inner divine blueprint, you will glow internally and externally. What you emit from your soul, is your real sexiness; your ability and conviction that you are a divine feminine, with a self awareness and full of purpose which creates freedom, peace and prosperity for you, those around you and the world.

Be your authentic self, reject false products that this system produces so that men don't get confused and fall into the trap, because the innocent unwanted (or wanted as a result of ignorance of self, not understanding the consequences of abusing sexual energy) children will suffer.

## S4 OXYGEN IS THE NUMBER ONE, ANYTHING ELSE IS SECONDARY

Nothing can survive without oxygen. Oxygen is the source of life. What you don't see without your eyes is what gives you 'life'. The ether or quantum field is where you come from.

"*Every living thing must breathe the air in order to live. The tree breathes the air through its leaves. The leaves are in this sense the lungs of the tree. Insects breathe air through tiny openings in their bodies. Frogs breathe the air partly through the skin. Fish breathe the air by taking oxygen out of the water as it passes over their gills. Man breathes the air through the air cells of the lungs*". – Frederick M. Rossiter

Our organs are brought to life through blood which is fed by oxygen. To keep physical and psychic balance and in good order, clean adequate oxygen is required. Most people only use a quarter or less part of the lung's surface.

Man came to physical existence a Perfect Breatharian. God (the Creator (not a physical being) breathed air in Man's nostrils and man became a living being/entity. Nothing was lacking to a breatharian Man (man and woman), and nothing more was needed. Simply by breathing, man was supplied with all requirements of animation. A Breatharian needs air only, and nothing else, to sustain his animated body. The moment we began ingesting external food and drinks, was the moment Man began degenerating.

Eating is just a habit, no different than smoking or drinking. Man thinks he needs to eat to survive and that is false. But of course, at the level that mankind (in actuality not so kind) is now, a slow incremental transition is required before someone is ready to live on just oxygen/ether. Later on, in the subject **S28**, *8 STEPS DIET – GRADUAL JOURNEY FROM DEATH TO LIFE* you will read about the different incremental steps one should take to go from de**gene**ration to re**gene**ration

As a society, we are focused too much on food and drinks. And yet, if air didn't exist, nothing else would matter. The air we breathe in the cities or in closed confinements is polluted. Even though it may seem that the body is doing fine no matter where you are, the body suffers damage from unclean/unhygienic air.

People who live in the mountains or other areas in nature away from smog, technological frequency and pollution, live longer than those who live in the pollution. Even if they consumed the same toxic products as those living in unclean air places, they would still live longer.

Whether you consume toxic products or just fruit and vegetables, you must still breathe adequate clean air. The earlier in the morning/rising, the better. Breathe as much as you can so that you can flood the blood and the brain with clean oxygen. Before going to bed at night, open the windows for a few minutes. You will be breathing all night whatever air is in the room.

"Man is like a breath, his days are but a fleeting shadow" – Psalm 144:4

Air/Oxygen is the original state of being. Modern Man is the degenerate descendant of the Breatharian. We are still alive (half dead) because Man's body had to adjust for survival throughout all the different levels from Breatharianism to Liquidarianism, then to Fruitarianism, to Vegetarianism, and finally the last and the lowest degenerative state which is Carnivorism.

Your lifespan depends on your breath quality (oxygen quality and breathing patterns). If you are someone who snores, you breathe more times than normal. Sleeping is supposed to be a healing state and not a marathon. Never breathe through your mouth, unless your nose is completely blocked of course. Animals breathe through the nose. People make fun of the animals or look down on animals, thinking that they are smarter than them. Sure, we have a rational mind, but what's the point of thinking when we fail even to the most basic universal lesson which is breathing properly. We are adults in body, but still children in the mind, our minds have been conditioned to wander on many external activities, or useless things which keeps us distracted from ourselves and from the present moment.

Usually, people tend to over-breathe (hyperventilate) and breathe through the mouth. The nose is a natural air conditioner. The nose filters humidity, heat, cold/freezing air before it reaches the lungs. Breathing through the mouth creates the potential for colds or disease. Why do you think our nostrils have hair? To filter it of course. When you breathe, you must use the full lung capacity, including the diaphragm. Breathing mainly from the diaphragm, uses only about 2% oxygen, while breathing from the upper chest muscles uses 25% oxygen. Most people fall into the 25% category.

> "Every fact of living existence, the Law of Vital Adjustment, the evidence contained in ancient scriptures, all prove without an exception that modern man is the product of descending Evolution–Devolution"
> - Hilton Hotema

Yogananda, in one of his books says that certain species that breathe fewer times per minute, tend to live longer than species who breathe a comparably greater number of times per minute.

- *A giant tortoise only takes four breaths per minute.*
- *Dogs take about 40-50 breaths per minute.*
- *An alligator while resting, is capable of taking only one breath per minute.*
- *Elephants only take four to five breaths per minute.*

Even though elephants and alligators don't live as long as a giant tortoise, they are certainly on the high-end of lifespan in the animal kingdom. Humans, on average, tend to take between 12 and 20 breaths per minute, which their life spans end up being between 60-100 years. Instead of wasting our time on social media, listening to many people's opinions, being distracted with what doesn't serve our soul's purpose, we should focus on ourselves, taking care of our body, mental and emotional state. Taking care of these requires deep slow and conscious breathing.

We can eat organic food all we want, we can research and gain a lot of knowledge, but if you fail to even breathe properly, we have failed our true selves, we have failed Divine Creation. Most people think they are alive, and yet, they are merely holding on to a thin thread where their death is hugging them tighter and tighter.

Every day, practice taking longer breaths. Practice daily and increase until you take only 5-10 breaths per minute. Use a watch or a clock to keep track. You can practice this immediately and achieve 5-10 breaths per minute but it will be forced. The point is that by practicing daily, and incrementally taking slower breaths, then it becomes a way of life, it becomes normal for you, by taking less and slower breaths per minute. Your mental and emotional state will improve, guaranteed. Try it and you will see. The breaths have to be conscious of course, while you are awake. But when you sleep, you take slow breaths anyway (unless you are having a nightmare and are scared in a dream).

If you manage (*I know you can do it if you want, anyone can*) to take 5 breaths per minute, then '*Breatharianism*' (living on just oxygen) will be achieved much faster.

Pay attention to your breathing patterns. Are they gentle or forceful, rapid or slow, deep or shallow? These send a crucial signal to your nervous system, telling it to be stressful or calm. Many people are stressed on a daily basis, by taking shallow and rapid breaths. Rapid breathing reduces oxygen efficiency, it increases heart rate. What this does is, it sends continuous signals to the brain that something is wrong, which consequently causes high levels of fatigue and anxiety.

# S5 LAST MEAL - NO LATER THAN 4PM

The later you eat dinner, the less energy the food has. The human body and everything else's energy function in direct proportion with the Sun's energy. When the Sun is down, no food should enter the human body. But why not eat after 4PM? This is just an example. It all depends on what you eat and what time of the year you are. The main reason to not eat late is because the longer the food stays in the rectum, the more potential for it to decay and damage the inner walls of the intestine.

Most people's intestines are loaded with decayed putrefied feces. What this does, it inhibits the body to properly absorb the nutrients, vitamins and the moisture of the food. People consume more unhygienic and toxic foods and drinks as it is, which they don't receive enough nourishment; where it creates havoc in the system where in the long run will create all kinds of diseases, early aging and consequently premature death.

One other thing, when the Sun is at its highest (noon-2Pm), that's when its energy is the most potent in digesting properly the food you eat. But what if it is cloudy? I would recommend that you eat less on cloudy days, but if you can fast, it is even better. Many times we eat at night, which we shouldn't, but what if we eat during the day, but in a room with closed curtains (especially when the curtains are very dark)? We should not eat in this case. Your eyes in the dark tell the system that it is dark, therefore the body's biological clock will get confused as it will go on Yin mode as opposed to Yang mode.

Many people nowadays stay up till late, destroy their body with snacks or even big meals, and then they wake up late and eat cooked products/snacks or heavy meals for breakfast. Little by little we must shed any attachment to foods, drinks, identifications with religions, political parties, false gods (false god=celebrities, public figures, political parties, materialism or any brand naming products etc.).

To know when to eat the last meal, we must know the digestion times. Water, juices and melons digest immediately, fruit takes 20-25minutes to digest. Vegetables take 40minutes. Processed foods such as bread, pasta, cooked food, pizza etc. take hours, with meat which takes the longest since humans have very long intestines as you will see later in **Subject 30**, '*13 physiological facts of humans' and animals' anatomy*'. To avoid any more complications, one should go to the bathroom as soon as the food is digested.

The end of the spinal cord is a bone like a hook which is arched toward the intestine. When you stand straight, that hook/coccyx or tailbone pinches the large intestine which stops the feces from falling out by themselves. If this intelligent design was not thought of, people would defecate while walking. At night, while sleeping, it is impossible to defecate because the human body is also equipped with the peristalsis function. Peristalsis is the wavelike contraction passing along the walls of the large intestine.

It is important that when you wake up (or any other time during the day when you know that you should have defecated by a certain time), go in the bathroom anyway and sit in the toilet. Rub the bottom of your belly in clockwise movements so that peristalsis is activated.

Previously I mentioned that it also depends on the season of the year. What I meant is that in the summer, the sun stays longer up in the sky (technically, the sun is always up 24/7, it's that from our point of view, it seems like the sun disappears in the evening), while in the winter goes to sleep earlier (again, the sun never sleeps, it just sleeps for you, but not for someone else in the other side of the world). Adjust your food consumption routine based on this principle/fact.

Here is one example, If you consume food that takes 4hours to digest (which means that at the end of that time, you must empty the digested food/feces), calculate that the food must not be eaten when the end of 4 hours is while you are asleep, otherwise, it will putrefy, and all night it will contribute to the damage of the body and the deformation of the large intestine.

If you sleep at midnight or 1AM, based on the logic above, you'd say, "Since it takes four hours for what I ate, then I'm going to eat around 9pm". Wrong, first of all, no food should be eaten when the sun is down, and secondly, it's much better that the last meal is consumed when the sun is at its height, energetically, which is at noon. After noon, the sun's energy slowly winds down until you don't see it anymore. The human body is perfectly mirrored with the energy of the sun.

## S6 NO SNACKS BETWEEN MEALS

Let me first begin by saying that we are created to not eat, nor drink anything external. We eat and drink because of the Law of Vital Adjustment. The body needs to adjust to survive, hence the current (since the degeneration began) society thinks/believes that it needs to eat. Eating is dying. There are two truths, two sides of the same coin. If you think that aging and dying is normal, then of course you'd think that eating is living. But, if you know and understand that we were not created to age nor die, then "**eating is living**" becomes "**eating is dying**".

A gradual process is required from degeneration to regeneration.

So, forget about living on just air for now. You can't do it now, even if you wanted to. Begin by consuming one less meal a day. Give your digestive system a much-needed break. What would happen if a car, bus, train, or an airplane worked nonstop without being taken care of? They would eventually break down. The same idea applies to your body. Fasting is the best way to fix the system, but before that, eat less meals a day.

Later on, you'll read about the Fasting Time Stamps. Why is it important to not consume snacks between meals? In the first hours after eating, as a result of the effects of insulin, your blood sugar decreases to near normal after spiking. And it typically doesn't continue climbing because insulin is immediately delivered into your circulatory system after eating. If you eat snacks, your insulin levels will begin to spike/rise again. Therefore, no snacks between meals. Even if you eat three meals a day (which is very bad), if you don't consume any snacks in between meals, it is much better.

Nowadays, people choke their bodies to death by consuming snacks all day. Even if the snack was a piece of carrot or an apple, it is bad, let alone consuming chips, chocolates, cookies or any of the other of the 1000+ disgusting death/toxic foods and drinks that are sold in stores.

## S7 WATER MUST NEVER BE CONSUMED WITH SOLID FOOD

When you put something in your mouth to eat, when you begin chewing, the mouth produces digestive enzymes to break out the food as best as possible before it enters the stomach. The stomach doesn't have teeth, so it relies on the digestive juices to further break down the food. If you drink water while eating, the water will wash out the enzymes, and the food will damage the stomach. The water immediately passes through the stomach and it also washes away any juices/secretions that are required to digest the food. It is common in the whole world where people eat and drink at the same time/on the same meal.

And on top of that, the water is harmful. Yes, I know, you must think I'm crazy. I said that because of the knowledge, understanding and the fact that we produce our own internal endogenous water. Any external water is harmful. Most people think water is life, because they compare themselves with how one feels without water. And they are right, because they are at that level (as I still am a bit) where they need the water, just because their body's ability to produce its own water is severely damaged.

Many people, especially children, consume cereal with milk. First of all, milk is meant for the baby of the cow. Only humans have been degenerated to a level where they think that it is okay to drink the milk of another species. Milk is liquid, that liquid will wash out the digestive enzymes so the cereals will damage the stomach lining and the whole system, since cereal is toxic. Just because people have been consuming it for decades doesn't mean that it must be consumed. I know that many people want to defend their beliefs about anything. I am simply presenting information. You can consume anything you want. It is your life, you are responsible for it.

## S8 COOKED FOOD IS DEAD FOOD, EVEN IF IT'S COOKED VEGETABLES

Not only that by consuming cooked food you don't absorb any nourishment from it, but what's even worse is when we consume cooked food from the previous day. This happens for various reasons such as, being born in poor countries, and to not waste food, we eat the meal from the day before. Even if we can afford to consume fresh food daily, we may still consume the dead food because it is transferred from the past, or from the parents since we were children. I, myself, had fallen for it. Many times I ate cooked food from the day before because I didn't want to waste it, because I was bombarded since I was a child to not throw food away.

Another reason is that because we have to work (depending on the job) we pack our lunch which contains the contents of the previous day's cooking. So, by having been conditioned to work like slaves, this system has turned a whole society into consuming harmful foods and drinks. In the case of drinks, I'm speaking of home-made fruit juice which is still not good if you consume it a few hours after it is made or the next day. This is because after a short while that the juice is made, when it comes in contact with the oxygen, it loses most of its nourishment qualities, no matter how good it tastes. And this is bad about the so-called food/drinks made home.

It's even worse if we consume foods and drinks that are processed and full of toxic chemicals which affect the nervous system. We are our nervous system/consciousness. There is no excuse for ignorance.

We cannot grow healthy if we don't nourish ourselves with life (raw *natural food).

*Everything is natural, even the toxic chemicals or any other poison; do not be deceived by the word "natural" written in food packaging you buy in the stores. The only natural food that exists is the one that grows on the ground (under and over it). Anything else that is processed and put in bottles or packages, is dead food.

>>>·<<<

*The way in which humans use plants, foods, and drugs cause the values of individuals and ultimately, whole societies to shift. Eating some foods makes us happy, eating others sleepy and still others alert. We are jovial, restless, aroused, or depressed depending on what we have eaten. Society tactically encourages certain behaviors that correspond to internal feelings, thereby encouraging the use of substances that produce acceptable behaviors.*

*Suppression of expression of sexuality, fertility and sexual potency, degree of visual acuity, sensitivity to sound, speed of motor response, rate of maturation, and lifespan – these are only some of an animal's characteristics that can be influenced by food plants with exotic chemistries. Human symbol formation, linguistic facility, and sensitivity to community values may also shift under the influence of psychoactive and physiologically active metabolites. A night spent observing behavior in a singles bar should be fieldwork enough to confirm this observation. Indeed the mate-getting hustle has always placed a high premium on linguistic facility, as perennial attention to patter styles and opening lines attests.* - Terence McKenna in ***Food of the Gods***, p.15

Almost all of us fail at this. We have been conditioned to indulge in food and drinks any time of the day, and many others eat at night when the Sun (which is the generator of the human digestive system) is sleeping (from your point of view/location in the world). Even if we didn't eat a lot, there are still refinements that have to be done, regarding when we must eat, how much we should eat and whether we can combine certain foods with others or not.

### ELECTRO-MAGNETIC BIO-CHEMICAL-RAYS

| ultraviolet | 2PM - MID DAY | yellow |
|---|---|---|
| purple | Normal Blood Pressure | orange |
| violet | | red |
| Blue | | scarlet |
| azure | | magenta |
| turquoise | | infrared |
| **9AM – 11AM** High Blood Pressure | 11AM - | **2PM – 5PM** Low Blood Pressure |

Ultraviolet sun rays hit the Earth at 9AM, and the other rays until 11AM consecutively. At 2PM, yellow rays hit the Earth and us, and then continue with the other rays (orange, red, scarlet, magenta and infra-red) until 5Pm. Unless the day is longer, depending on the season, then the times are stretched out. Regardless of the seasons, midday is always midday, from 11AM to 2Pm (pertaining to the ideal time when someone should eat). Three hours out of 24, is the ideal time to consume solid food, until you are ready for the "Liquidarianism" step. For the rest of the steps check **S28** titled, '8 STEPS DIET – GRADUAL JOURNEY FROM DEATH TO LIFE".

The next best time to eat is from 9 AM to 11AM. Train yourself to not consume solid food after 2PM, and definitely not after the Sun sets. Before practicing this, I was eating at 6 or 7 Pm. Even though the Sun had not set yet, it was still not the ideal time to consume solid food. Our digestive system works in tandem with the powerful energy of the Sun, the higher up the sun is in the sky, the more potent its energy and vice versa. This should also reflect our eating habits/ choices.

The point is to eat when the body is in the normal blood pressure state from 11AM to 2PM. A lot of people drink coffee (as an example). Based on the above table (which is a physiological, energetical and astrological fact), do you think is it okay to consume a product which raises or lowers your blood pressure? The choice is always yours to make. Don't wait until it is too late. Salt also messes up your blood pressure. The only real salt a.k.a. sodium that is assimilated by the body, is found in fruit and vegetables. Even the sweet fruit has sodium in it.

Currently, and as it has been for a very long time (from the time that our species began degenerating), people eat because they feel like they would die if they didn't, and that is true for some (most of us) that have damaged their bodies for decades from indulging in all the garbage that this system produces. The source of all is invisible, in this case, the cosmic rays are what truly nourishes us.

What do all the textbooks on anatomy teach? They teach that the human body is composed of trillions of cells. All the cells are not composed of food. Science has proved and admitted that the Parent Cell is not the product of food. Food does not and cannot preserve a cell. A cell's main food is "cosmic rays". In this chapter I'm writing about the ideal time when one should eat. But this is the next step in the journey to perfect health. The change must be gradual.

If you eat every day, you can't just live on oxygen for weeks and months if you decide to abruptly stop eating; your body will fail. Sure, you can dry fast for a day or two, but eventually your body will suffocate, it needs the food in accordance with its current state. Eating solid food is not about living, but about lasting a little bit longer before death knocks at your door. If you want to live, one must gradually practice the 8 steps of diet which I wrote about in this book, with the 8th step being Breatharianism (living on just air/oxygen/ ether).

The Parent Cell's origin is a mystery. Could its origin be from the invisible world/the Great MIND?

Hilton Hotema in his book, *"Man's Higher Consciousness"* wrote: *"Whence come the Cell? Or the materials of which they are composed?*

*They rise as shadows and become substance as the result of the condensation and materialization of Cosmic Rays. That substance is not food. It constitutes the elements of the Universe that have always existed and are eternal. As the so-called seed of the parents come near to each other, certain elements of each stand out separately and come nearer. These separate, individual particles merge and fuse as they were into each other, producing a clear field in which nothing appears. Finally, after a period of seeming quiescence, granulation occurs at a point between the places occupied by the gametes of the parents when they merged, fused and disappeared from sight. When the so-called seed of the parent meet and fuse, they thus create a condition or electro-magnetic center, which is necessary for the occurrence of the phenomenon that produces man's body. That center attracts cosmic rays, of a definite frequency, corresponding to the chemistry of the center. The rays crystalize around the center in the form of similar substance; and man comes into physical being under a magic process of transformation of invisible elements into visible form"*

## S10 INTERMITTENT FASTING

Intermittent fasting is when you alternate between periods of eating and fasting. This type of eating is often described as "patterns," "cycles" or "schedules" of fasting. Intermittent fasting isn't about starving yourself — it's about cutting way back on calories for short time periods. You can drink water and tea during fasting periods, but not honey in the water or the tea or any other beverages. Later on, when you read about the fasting time stamps, you'll understand why consuming honey raises the sugar levels in the blood.

The belief is that your body becomes satisfied with smaller portions while also reducing cravings for unhealthy snack foods. That is, as long as you maintain a healthy diet while trying it all out. There are several effective approaches, but it all comes down to personal preference, assuming your preference doesn't include satisfying your cravings. If you want to give intermittent fasting a try, be prepared to figure out what works best for you, it might take some trial and error first.

Some people find it easy to fast for 16 hours and confine meals to just eight hours of the day, such as 9 a.m. to 5 p.m., while others have a hard time and need to shorten their fasting window. No matter what you do, you must push harder than you think you can.

If you don't fast, you will make sure to eat your way to death. Perhaps death is not concerning you in the present moment. One day, when your organs begin to fail you will regret your past choices. Why not think ahead, why not steer the ship towards the open horizon as opposed to a dead-end wall? You either choose death or life. By practicing the fine art of fasting you will extend your lifespan. You will be in charge of your human physical, mental and emotional temple.

There are many levels of fasting. One must gradually practice the levels. As a beginner, assuming you are one, begin with short fasts, one day a week without eating any solid food, but drink plenty of water. Your system deserves a day off don't you think? If you make your inner cells (which are your workers) work 7 days a week, then you'd be a bad boss wouldn't you?

## S11 WET/WATER FASTING

By wet fasting I mean water fasting or juicing which is still fasting but not as good as water fasting. It is not as good, having in mind that the juice still has fruit particles which technically would not allow the body to achieve autophagy, but don't be concerned with autophagy for now. You'll get there after you become strong enough to fast for at least 24 hours on just water, without forcing yourself. Have in mind that the ideal optimal juice fasting is when you juice at home and not drinking store bought fruit juice.

Water ages you, but please bear with me, depending on the level that you are, water may be crucial to your survival. The knowledge is scattered everywhere in this book. There are different steps or levels to health; when you understand that we were born to not age nor die, that we are only meant to live on just oxygen, then will the "*water ages you*" make sense. But for now, if you are not already a breatharian or if you are not living on just home-made fruit juices, then water is a must, until you get to the next step.

Water fasting is actually a "*water diet*". Water flows, water does not resist. When you put your hand on or under it, it caresses you. The same applies for your body, water caresses your organs and every one of your trillions of cells. Water will never be a solid wall, it will never stop you, it will only go where it needs to go, for as long as it is alive water (free of pollution). Most water you purchase in stores is dead water, devoid of life. There are devices out there that can zap the water and give it a high natural frequency, as if it was spring water from the mountains.

While fasting on just water, since it is not the best water out there, make sure you help your body also by breathing fresh air. Many people wake up in the rising and stay in bed, scrolling on their cell phone for an hour or two. Use that time to open the windows so that the room gets fresh air, and get out on the balcony or on the porch and breathe that fresh air. The air contains the most vital component of life.

Water fasting requires a clean environment and no stress, no TV or Internet (since you'd see content that would get you to crave foods and drinks and other harmful activities). You should take sunbaths, walk in nature, listen to healing music, conscious deep breathing, previous fasting experience. You must practice juice fasting before attempting water fasts. Never break the fast with solid food, and definitely no cooked food. When you fast, the internal system/organs becomes like a child's organs, soft, and sensitive. You will do much more damage if you break the fast with bad solid food than if you don't fast at all. Avoid sexual activity while fasting, until full strength has returned. Technically, chaste life is the ideal state but you may not be ready for that level yet.

## S12 WATER AGES YOU

What? Water ages you? This is madness, how could it be? It is important to go beyond what is deemed normal. Water is important but only when you consume anything besides raw natural food (fruit). Water is needed to flush the toxins out. But if you only consume raw natural food that grows on the ground, then water is not needed. It is not as simple as it seems and yet it can be simple when we take care not just of our body but also of our mind. The fruit and vegetables provide any vitamins, nutrients, organic minerals/cell salts that  the body needs. Even if you only consume fruit and vegetables, you must still practice continence (semen and ovum retention).

The human body is a machine with many cogs (muscles, heart, spinal cord and cerebrospinal fluid), endocrine system, gut, heart, brain/nervous system etc. Which means that raw food and vegetables is not enough. A lot of toxic food/drinks eaters (including meat eaters) make fun or dismiss the veganism*. That's because they hold on to their beliefs that humans are carnivores, which is a fallacy because anatomy/physiology of animal meat eaters prove that humans clearly are not carnivores, which you will read later in the subject 13 Biological Facts about humans/animals.

Water is a must, for as long as you consume anything other than fruit and vegetables, especially fruit which contain the next best water, beside the *endogenous water, which is the best water, which the body produces by itself when it is in a state of balance and harmony. That state of balance and harmony will eventually and finally happen when you become a breatharian. Water is not needed when your blood is not acidic anymore from all the refined flour and sugar products, including coffee, alcohol, tea, meat and many other processed foods and drinks.

*endogenous* – *Occurring within the physical body as a normal part of metabolism*. Most people's bodies are severely damaged where barely any endogenous water is created, hence the need for external water.

Most of the water which the world population consumes, causes ossification of the arteries. The blood is 90% water. The blood is what supplies the rest of the body. If the blood is polluted, so will the rest of the body be. Hence, the blood is called the river of life. If a river is dirty, it will pollute the ocean. People give great attention to what they eat, but not to what they drink. The city water is polluted constantly and people are like crickets, without protesting. Protesting doesn't mean going in the streets asking for healthy water and food. Protesting means to stop consuming the poison they give you. They only care about money, if you don't buy their poison, they will have no choice but to listen or to leave us alone. They capitalize on people being ignorant.

Water contains inorganic minerals (with the exception of distilled water). The inorganic minerals are unassimilable and they settle in the body as calcareous deposits. Over time, these calcareous deposits harden the arteries. Hardening of the arteries means less space for blood to efficiently go through. When the arteries are hardened, cholesterol attaches to those parts for the purpose of saving you. But the more cholesterol attaches in those parts, the smaller the arteries become to the point that even if one doesn't have a heart attack, all their organs and their brain will receive less amount of blood. One way or another, disease and death will be a certainty.

There is nothing wrong with cholesterol. The cholesterol is doing its job to protect you, but too much hardening of the arteries will attract more cholesterol. We can't blame cholesterol just like we can't' blame a runny nose, snot or phlegm. They are doing their job in expelling the toxins out of the body. Never take cholesterol medicine. Any man-made medicine is toxic. What one should do, is to stop consuming what made them sick in the first place which is, bad food, bad drinks, not enough sun, no contact with nature, no exercise, man-made medications, stress, worries etc. The healing begins from within.

Water (clean purified one) is life. Many people, especially in the western countries, live on a mostly dry solid diet. Your body is over 70% water. We must consume food that is at least 70% water – "As above So below". The Earth's waters (oceans/seas) are over 70% water. Over seventy percent of your daily consumption must be food that contains water, and that is vegetables which contain over 70% water and most fruit which contain 70% - over 90% water such as in the case of watermelon and grapes.

# S13 DRY FASTING – ENDOGENOUS WATER CREATION

First of all, after you read this subject, make sure you also read the subject "WHO SHOULD NOT FAST" which is a few subjects later. There are two types of dry fasting: **soft dry fast** and **hard dry fast**.

**A soft dry fast** allows you to be in contact with water, like bathing, washing your hand and face but DO NOT swallow any water, as that would cancel the fast, even if you drank the purest water that exists.

**A hard dry fast** requires no contact with any water. This type of dry fast is NOT recommended. But if you want to read about it and dry fasting in general, check the book that I mentioned in this chapter.

While you practice dry fasting, do not brush your teeth. The water that you use to brush your teeth with, will feed the parasites and pathogens. You don't want to undo your progress. When you know which days you will practice dry fasting, have a shower the day before. If for whatever reason you get dirty or really sweaty and you need a shower, then have a shower of course. It's common sense that hygiene is important too. It is better to have the knowledge rather than not. You decide what you do with it. You may be asking yourself (actually I like to put questions in your mind):

*"Even If I don't brush my teeth, water will enter my body when I wash my hands, do the dishes or wash my face, how would not brushing my teeth make a difference?"*

My answer to that is, your skin is the biggest organ in the body, anything that goes into your skin goes into your system, but under the tongue the skin is the thinnest which means that water immediately penetrates the skin. But as long as you don't ingest any water, the dry fast will not be canceled. Do not get panicked by this subject. Dry fasting is for those who are already intermediate or expert in fasting. When you sleep at night, you are dry fasting anyway, the only difference with dry fasting when you are awake is that you are conscious of your decision, the whole universe bends to your will in improving your overall health. You may have another question about brushing your teeth:

**YOU** - "What if you have a bad breath?"
**ME** - Good question, ask yourself what is the reason that you have bad breath?
**YOU** – My teeth are fine, no cavities, but I still need to brush my teeth.
**ME** – Your teeth are fine, aren't they? Good, here is the next question that I'll ask. "If your teeth are fine, don't you think that perhaps the bad breath is a result of your stomach/internal body/s filth?

Now we are getting somewhere. Your stomach/internal organs were meant to be a place of intuition, a place where your aspiration and resonance catapulted you to a more powerful self-awareness state. Your stomach was never meant to become a sewage system. You are a living being, your body must be fed with life and not with dead foods, dead drinks and dead/distorted thoughts. All these forms of deaths create energy stagnation.

Energy is meant to flow and not be trapped. No matter what you do, make sure that no water enters your mouth including juices, or even breath. "No breath" means not breathing through your mouth but instead only through your nose. The air has moist/water. The ether should provide you with the needed moisture, which in turn, your body will produce its own endogenous water.

In the book, **The Phoenix Protocol** by August Dunning, the author says:

> "The Russian doctors, who perfected dry fasting, determined that the only stipulation is that no water enters the gastrointestinal tract via the mouth. They found that drinking water stimulates gastric juices and stops the transition to endogenous nutrition. Drinking water during a fast, also prevents the blood from becoming concentrated which then can't stimulate the hypothalamus to start endogenous water production. Bathing is recommended and takes advantage of the skin's ability to absorb water in a type of counter flow into the skin. This method improves the ability of the body to flush toxins out of the extracellular matrix into the lymphatic system without gastrointestinal tract involvement". - August Dunning, The Phoenix Protocol

There are two cardinal rules that cannot be violated during a fast. These are critical physiological conditions that must be maintained:

**1**- *Blood glucose levels must be maintained because the brain and red blood cells absolutely depend on glucose for fuel to stay alive.*

**2**- *Vital proteins in the heart and skeletal muscles must be protected to prevent loss of function.*

Dry fasting obeys the cardinal rules. Unless you dry fast, your body will never produce the full amount of endogenous needed internal water/life, which means that external water will be needed to survive (but death will still arrive). When/if you dry fast, try to breathe as much as you can clean/fresh air, it is the molecules in the air/ether that feeds your cells. Even scientifically it has been proven that the cells are not and cannot rely on external foods and drinks. Which means that food is useless. We eat because our bodies have been degenerated, but we can regenerate if we improve our health step by step until all we need is ether. We are born from ether.

Many times, we feel like we need to spit, but every single drop of moisture is vital to the body, when you dry fast, do not spit, unless you have phlegm, which in that case you wouldn't want to dry fast anyway.

## S14 EKADASHI fasting–THE ELEVENTH DAY

The word "Ekadashi" derives from Sanskrit. Ekadashi is a Hindu fast observed/practiced on the eleventh day after the full moon or the new moon where your body does not demand food.

The study of Vedic astronomy has revealed the significance of the position of the moon and its influence on the human mind. One complete moon cycle lasts approx. 28 days. That means that there is around 14 days between the new moon and the full moon. Ekadashi, literally meaning *"eleventh"*, is the eleventh day of the lunar fortnight. Every month there are two Ekadashi, exactly eleven days after the full and new moon.

Exactly 4 days before the two lunar cycles of the month, called **Krishna Paksha** (new moon) and **Shukla Paksha** (waxing moon), this day is auspicious for the mind to be in its natural state of wisdom.

According to **Ayurveda**, if you fast on Ekadashi's day, what you consumed that day will have an effect on your body **after 4 days.** So they are good days to cleanse the system, rest the digestive system, realign the body, purify the mind, stay energized, and avoid lethargy.

For more on Ekadashi fasts, check on YouTube or simply read this article about 24 types of Ekadashi fasts.

https://www.pranawakening.com/post/24-ekadashis-how-to-do-the-fasting

## S15 JUICE FASTING

Juice fasting is great, and very beneficial. Of course, depending on where you are at the moment on your healing journey and capability, you may not be ready for fasting on just juices yet, or you may be beyond this level. But if you can fast on just water, then juice fasting is super easy. Juice fasting is not really a true fast but a **liquid**arian elimination diet. If you are a first timer, this is the first step in fasting on liquids. While practicing this kind of fast, you can also work, because this fasts supplies you with calories and nutrition, unlike water fasting which it doesn't.

In our current state, we'd be lucky to digest 70% of the fruit and vegetables, but when you consume the juice, you assimilate at least 90% of it, even if you have a weak digestion system. In certain countries where the Western food industry mafia doesn't have much power, they treat (actually cure) cancer patients with fruit or green leafy juices. Do not fall for supplement/vitamin pills scams. They are dead food, they have been treated with heat and chemical solvents. There is nothing better than the juice from natural fresh fruit.

> "This is the whole concept behind a vitamin pill: a concentration of nutrients in a pill. But it is not the same thing. Vitamins involve several steps of processing along the journey from a fresh food into a tablet. Many of those steps may involve heat, which destroys or alters nutrients. Chemical solvents may also be involved. Or, of course, the nutrients may not even be natural at all but synthetic. Manufacturing tablets and capsules involves adding ingredients other than the active ingredient. These are called excipients. They can be anything from sweeteners, to stabilizers, coloring agents, fillers, talc, binders etc. If you are trying to heal, choose live food; the juice of living plants".
> - STEVE MEYEROWITZ, *Juice Fasting*

When you consume only fruit juices for a long time, at one point you may lose some hair. What falls is dead cells, but just like anything else in the body, the hair will regrow and never fall again (no gray hair either, no matter the age) if you are consistent in your journey to complete health. There is a transitioning period, like giving birth to a child. Which means pain. Transitioning means a length of time. If your body is filthy, you cannot cleans yourself in one day.

The filthier the body is, the more painful will the beginning of the transition be, but it is a requirement for the next step. Just like you exercise to build muscles, so will you have to put the effort in improving your overall health.

## S16 NUT JUICE (NOT MILK). ALMONDS DON'T HAVE TITTIES

Steve Meyerowitz in his book (which was mentioned earlier), Juice Fasting & Detoxification says:

*"If you are desiring food early on in your fast and are having trouble with your hunger, or if you are on a long term – over 30 days – Liquidation regime, nut milks are for you. These high protein drinks are rich and perfect for when cravings or protein needs exist. They should not be used regularly in short fasts because they are too concentrated and may increase the desire for solid food. They are perfect in the beginning for settling into your fast, on long fasts to carry you through and for coming out of a fast".*

Steve uses the word 'milk', but I don't use the word milk to describe anything that doesn't come from the breasts. The word 'milk' is a marketing term to get people to buy their products. Most nut juices (which are labeled as milk) sold in stores are very harmful, they are loaded with chemicals. The best nut juice you can have is to make it yourself at home. To make your own nut juice you can use almonds, walnuts, pecans, hazelnuts, macadamia nuts, or cashew nuts. Simply blend 1 cup of the nut of your choice with 3 and a half cup of water. You can add a teaspoon of honey or maple syrup.

Know that when you make nut juice, there will still be very tiny particles of nuts/powder, so it won't be pure fast. But depending on your level, you decide whether you are ready for water only fast or if you want to gradually go from smoothies for a few days, then onto nut juices and then onto water fasting. There is no *'one size fits all'*. No matter what you read here or anywhere else, listen to your body, especially to your intuition. Your body a.k.a. your stomach may tell you that you need food, but it doesn't mean that you need to eat. Understand that you are not your body, listen to your intuition first. If you don't, then eventually you will have no choice but to hear your body whisper and then scream (pain, diseases and surgeries).

# S17 FASTING TIME STAMPS

Here is a breakdown of the hourly fasting benefits that Saimir Kercanaj wrote in the book "***BODY MIND SOULS – AS YOU BELIEVE SO SHALL IT BE***".

**0h - 2h BLOOD SUGAR RISES**. You will feel normal during the first hours of fasting because your body is going through the regular process of breaking down glycogen (a form in which glucose is stored in muscle and liver tissue. In other words, it's the substance that is deposited in bodily tissues as a store of carbohydrates). Your blood sugar rises. Your pancreas releases insulin to break down glucose for energy (innerG) and stores the extra glucose for later whenever it's needed.

**2h - 5h BLOOD SUGAR FALLS**. As a result of the effects of insulin, your blood sugar decreases to near normal after spiking. And it typically doesn't continue climbing because insulin is immediately delivered into your circulatory system after eating. Don't forget to avoid snacks as your sugar levels will rise again if you do.

**5h - 8h BLOOD SUGAR RETURNS TO NORMAL**. At this stage, your blood sugar levels return to normal. Feeling hungry? Your body is reminding you that it's been a while since your last meal. However, you are not actually that hungry. Starve to death, shrivel up and lose your muscle mass? None of this is going to happen. Actually, your glycogen reserves will begin to fall, and you might even lose a little body fat. Your body will continue to digest your last food intake. It starts to use stored glucose for energy and continues to function as if you will eat again soon.

**8h - 10h SWITCH INTO FASTING MODE.** 8 hours after your last meal, your liver will use up the last of its glucose reserves. Now your body goes into a state called gluconeogenesis, which indicates that your body has switched into the fasting mode. Studies show that gluconeogenesis, a metabolic pathway, results in the generation of glucose from body fat instead of carbohydrates. It increases your calorie burning.

**10h - 12h BARELY ANY GLYCOGEN LEFT**. The glycogen reserves are running out. As a result, you may become irritable or hungry. Just relax, it is a sign that your body is burning fat. With little glycogen left, fat cells (adipocyte) will release fat into your bloodstream. They

26

also go straight into the liver and are converted into energy for your body. Actually, you are cheating your body into burning fat in order to survive.

**12h - 18h KETOSIS STATE**. Now it's the turn of fat to fuel your body. You are in the metabolic state called ketosis. The glycogen is almost used up and your liver converts fat into ketone body - an alternative energy source for your body. Fat reserves are readily released and consumed. For this reason, ketosis is sometimes referred to as the body's fat-burning mode. Ketosis produces fewer inflammatory by-products, so it provides health benefits to your heart, metabolism, and brain.

**18h - 24h FAT BURNING MODE BEGINS**. The longer you fast, the deeper into ketosis you'll go. By 18 hours, your body has switched into fat-burning mode. Research shows that after fasting for 12-24 hours, the energy supply from fat will increase by 60%, and it has a significant increase after 18hours
.

1-The level of ketone bodies rises.

2-Ketones act as signaling molecules to tell your body how to better regulate its metabolism in a stressful environment.

3-Your body's anti-inflammatory and rejuvenation processes are ready to work.

**24h - 48h AUTOPHAGY BEGINS**. At this point, your body triggers autophagy (which means self-devouring). Cells start to clean up their house. They remove unnecessary or dysfunctional components. It allows the orderly degradation and recycling of cellular components. During autophagy, cells break down viruses, bacteria, and damaged components. In this process, you get the energy to make new cell parts. It is significant for the cell's health, renewal, and survival. The main benefit of autophagy is best known as the body turning the clock back and creating younger cells. Which means by fasting from this level to 72h fasting, you slow down or stop aging.

**48h - 56h GROWTH HORMONE GOES UP**. Your growth hormone level is much higher than the level at which it was before fasting. This benefits from the ketone bodies production and hunger hormone secretion during fasting. Growth hormone helps increase your lean muscle mass and improves your cardiovascular health.

**56h -72h SENSITIVE TO INSULIN**. Your insulin is at its lowest level since fasting. It makes you more insulin sensitive, which is an especially good thing if you have a high risk of developing diabetes. Lowering your insulin levels has a range of health benefits both short and long term, such as activating autophagy and reducing inflammation.

**72h - CONGRATULATIONS** if you made it this far (both in reading and fasting for 72h). IMMUNE CELLS REGENERATE
"Survival of the fittest." Your body turns down cellular survival pathways and recycles immune cells that are damaged when fighting viruses, bacteria, and germs. In order to fill the recycled/not available cells, your body regenerates new immune cells at a rapid pace. It starts the immune system regeneration and shifts cells to a state of self-renewal. Your immune system becomes stronger and stronger. Do you now innerstand how important fasting is?

The act of fasting, triggers a switch to flip in the body, signaling it to begin a 'stem-cell based regeneration of the hematopoietic system.' It requires the body to utilize up its stores of glucose, fat, ketones, as well as starting to break down a large number of white blood cells. The loss of white blood cells flags the body, in turn, restores brand-new immune system cells.

## S18 WHO SHOULD NOT FAST?

Fasting is very important but not everyone should fast, especially long (24h, 36h, 72h etc.) fasting sessions. Many people's system is fractured severely, where even a good healthy habit may harm them. No matter what, train yourself to admit that your body needs to improve where you must take actions in allowing the body to fix itself through the right diet (according to each individual's need) and the right activities (sun gazing/bathing, grounding, meditation, deep breathing techniques etc.)

*Some people who should not fast (unless they undertake fasting under professional supervision) are:*

| Those who are | Those who are |
|---|---|
| Diabetics | Underweight |
| Nursing moms | Advanced heart disease |
| Pregnant women | Kidney disfunction |
| Most hypoglycemics | Critically ill |
| Most elderly | On long term medication |
| Growing children | Have tuberculosis |

There are exceptions to anything, but to be sure, if you fall in one of these categories, it's better if you consult a health (homeopathic) professional. Unless you are like me, where I am my own doctor and scientist. Nonetheless, you know your body better than me, so act accordingly.

## S19 EYES – THE WINDOWS OF THE SOUL

While I was driving, I visualized light/energy travelling from my root chakra going all the way to my pineal gland. Every time I do this, my eye-sight improves. In the distance I see everything blurry. I did this with my eyes open because I was driving. But if you can't visualize something else to what your eyes are seeing, then visualize with your eyes closed. Technically, your eyes never close, your eyelids do.

The eyes are connected with the liver. Anger harms the liver. When the liver is not functioning optimally, it can affect the eyesight. The eyesight can be affected by many factors, but 3 major factors are:

1- Incontinence (overindulgence in sexual activity through sexual intercourse, masturbations and orgasms). Your semen or ovum (including any secretions that are wasted through arousal, masturbation, orgasm or sex) contains your life force. If you waste your life force, there will be less lifeforce in certain parts of the body, especially the brain, since phosphorus in this case, is the main component that gives brain health.

2- Aye strain by looking at a specific distance for a long time on a daily basis such as, phones, tablets, computer monitors etc.

3- Anger (such as in my case, until I overcame it for good).

Emotions have a big impact on our health. The internal organs are damaged over time when we get angry, worried, when we grieve over time, or when we live in a fearful state.

**These emotions weaken these major organs:**

Anger weakens the liver
Stress weakens the heart and the brain
Worry weakens the stomach
Grief weakens the lungs
Fear weakens the kidneys

If any of these 6 organs fails, your life is forfeited. Living like a walking zombie is not a life. That's why we must put effort in not abusing our body, mind and spirit, or else we may end up dead or in a wheelchair.

-Fluorine is an organic mineral, one of the 12 essential minerals that is needed for optimal health. This mineral exists in fruit and vegetables, herbs and nuts. All the 12 minerals exist in abundance in natural raw food that grows on the ground. Fluorine is an important component of the enamel of the teeth and the iris of the eye.
-The Sun is the number one solution to fix your eyesight. Even if it's winter, look at the Sun on a cloudy day. Find where the Sun is located and look at it, only if it's fully or half covered by the clouds, otherwise do not look directly at it but around it for a few seconds with your eyes open without blinking, and repeat also while blinking.

In my case, I consume mostly fruit and vegetables. I have been practicing sexual alchemy which also means semen retention for a while, so the only thing that I thought could be the problem was my liver since I was an angry person often, for a very specific reason. The reason is this decayed deceptive system/Matrix. I know the solution to many things which I had to validate through personal experience. But when I try to bring self-awareness to people I know in real life, they are too lazy to even listen to me, let alone research, understand and then apply said knowledge. And stuff like this angered me. I'm not angry with them but with the whole thing/system.

Being awake, thinking for yourself is both a blessing and a curse. So, all the anger affects the liver. Depending on the severity of each individual, the damage can be bad or not so bad. In my case it's energetic. I don't drink alcohol or any other man-made drink. It is very important to understand that we are energy. Energy imbalance is the only disease that truly exists. Everything we think, say, do, eat, and drink, affects our auric field, our consciousness - our life.

## S20 ALCOHOL & LEGAL DRUGS, – THE UNSEEN MONSTERS DISGUISED AS 'FEELING GOOD'

As far as things that you ingest I will use only three types of legal drugs. But there are thousands upon thousands of products that people consume daily which are deemed legal and yet all those products are killing people.

<u>Alcohol – SOUL SNATCHER</u>

In page 62, in the book *Creation Of The Superman* by Dr. Raymond Bernard (with commentary by Liquid Metal), the author says:

*"Alcohol, in any quantity and in any form, either as whiskey, wine or beer, poisons the heart, liver, kidneys and nervous system, arousing morbid sex tendencies and causing a gradual degeneration of the brain. The drinking of much alcohol produces marked effects; the taking of a small quantity leads to less noticeable ones. The latter, if accumulated for a sufficient length of time, will, however, make themselves manifest in the form of pathological and degenerative processes. Senile dementia (which is an aggravated form of ordinary senility) is such an after-effect of chronic alcoholism. The use of alcohol causes heart failure, hardening of the arteries, liver and kidney diseases, rheumatism, obesity, high blood pressure and insanity. The pathological effects of alcohol, especially when old age approaches, are very similar to those of meat, except that they are more severe. General physical and mental degeneration, with marked waning of the intellectual faculties, are the final results of the alcohol habit".*

On two different occasions, I have heard people asking in the restaurant for vegan wine. This is 100% conflicting. We cannot improve if we keep lying to ourselves. To ask for vegan alcohol, even though the liquid is not alcohol (at least, it's what I think), it means that the thought pattern (or low vibration entity) of alcohol is still in the mind. So, by asking for vegan alcohol we are lying to ourselves. Why would you want alcohol in the first place? If we want to consume natural/vegan food or drinks, then what's the point of looking for it in the wrong place?

Unless someone was so addicted to alcohol and they are slowly transitioning to a natural food/drink lifestyle. Then, in this case, we can make an exception. Not everyone is strong enough to make a big change all of a sudden. But as long as we progress, even if the progress is slow, it is still respectable and honorable for putting in the effort. The same logic applies to decaffeinated coffee.

# S21 Coffee – STUNS YOUR PSYCHIC ABILITIES
Speaking of coffee, when I used to work for a corporation I was drinking coffee every day. So, I would stop and order one at a "drivethrough" [driving beside the building, order, drive a bit more

and pay and receive the coffee outside of the window – for those who live in countries that don't have or don't know what a drive through is]. What I would do sometimes is, I would pay for my coffee but I would also pay for the next person that was behind me in line. This is to let you know that you can do little things like this and you can make someone else's day. Other people have done this to me where they paid for my coffee. Don't expect someone else to do it first. You be the 1$^{st}$ one and set a trend. Just as being selfish and greedy can be contagious, so does being altruist, helping others can be contagious.

When you drink coffee you tend to want to pee much earlier than when you don't. That is because the cells do not allow coffee (which is a neurotoxin) in them. Yes, there is water in coffee, cells allow only endogenous water but because the water is polluted with caffeine/coffee, the system/body sees the whole thing as poison. But even if you are someone who doesn't drink coffee but still goes very frequently in the bathroom, it means that the body is polluted so much with toxins (even if on the surface you may look healthy) that it doesn't properly absorb the water. Any water not absorbed by the cells, will be rejected. In this book I have mentioned that cells don't rely on external foods or drinks, but that was related to breatharianism.

Since most people's bodies are polluted, according to the **Law of Vital Adjustment**, water (including food) is needed. Seeing the bigger picture helps us understand. By not seeing the bigger picture, some information here will seem conflicting, but as an author I like to express myself from different layers of thinking because not all who read this book are on the same level.

Coffee cuts more than 50% of the oxygen that is needed for the brain. Coffee doesn't give more energy; it simply fools the brain. After a few hours, it wears off and you can feel miserable. It was a false energy supply. You will then need to recover from the caffeine buzz so what do you do when that happens? You drink more to gain the energy back. It is an ongoing consumption of coffee that coffee drinkers fall for. I was a big coffee drinker. I drink coffee once a month but not because I need it. I just like the taste of it. When you consume something because you feel you need it, then that is an indication that it has become an addiction. But very soon, I will stop drinking coffee.

*"Detoxification is not a system of treatment*
*or a way to remove symptoms; it is a system*

*of curing by addressing the cause of the
disease. It involves the understanding that
the body is the healer, and that energy is
at the core of healing. It also sheds light
on the true cause of disease, the destruction
of energy. Energy or the destruction of energy
results from what we eat, drink, breathe, put
on our skin, and from what we think and feel.
These are the six ways we either make
ourselves healthy and vital, or sick and
weak."* - Robert Morse, N.D.

Some people can't begin the day unless they have coffee. If we need coffee to start living, we lack life purpose, which makes us lack motivation. We are already batteries, we don't need anything external to start or keep going. When you drink coffee [when someone is a regular drinker], the ability to feel tired is blocked because of caffeine. Coffee tricks you into thinking you are fine and that you don't need to do anything to improve your health. But in the long run, the glands of the body, the nervous system, the blood and the brain are damaged. Medications also block the ability to know you are sick. We shouldn't mask a condition with an illusion.

Liquid Metal, in the book **Creation of the Superman** by Dr. Raymond W. Bernard says:

*"If you just have one cup of coffee per day, in one year alone, you will add 255,500 unneeded/unnecessary extra beats to your heart. These beats will be taken out of your life force/lifespan reservoir. Unless you are already a superman or a superwoman, having a cup of coffee per day will shave off years of your life. All of us, when we are young and without any health problems, tend to dismiss, ridicule or deny information that could help us avoid future death/early aging. We think, just because we don't have any pain in the moment, we are fine. But the damage that unhealthy eating and drinking cause is accumulative. The consequences of coffee drinking are detrimental compared to the so-called its benefits".*

I just recalled a place I used to work at many years ago. Before even starting work, the boss would tell us to drink coffee before doing anything. He offered coffee for free every rising [morning]. He would offer it in a way that it seemed like he cared about the workers until we [some of the workers] figured out that he wanted us to start working at full speed. He cared about profit and nothing else, but it was a good experience. Everything is an experience and a lesson for as long as we learn from it.

If you were to search about, whether coffee or anything else is healthy or not, you'd find articles that are pro coffee but also those that are against it. By ignorance or not willing to let go of addictions, our ego tries to defend our beliefs to the point that we develop cognitive dissonance.

## S22 COFFEE EXPERIMENT ON SPIDERS – IMAGINE HOW BAD IT IS FOR HUMANS WITH AN ADVANCED NERVOUS SYSTEM

A NASA tech briefing *"Using Spider-Web Patterns To Determine Toxicity"* was published in April 1995. The work was done by researchers at Marshall Space Flight Center to see how various substances — including caffeine — affect spider web patterns. According to the briefing, the purpose of the study was to examine how toxic a chemical is by exposing spiders to it and comparing how their webs differed from that of a normal spider web.

The researchers exposed spiders to a range of different chemicals, including caffeine, marijuana, and Benzedrine — a type of amphetamine — and noted how they spun their webs under the influence of each of those substances. The experiment was performed on European garden spiders. The article noted:

> "It appears that one of the most telling measures of toxicity is a decrease, in comparison with a normal web, of the numbers of completed sides in the cells: the greater the toxicity, the more sides the spider fails to complete."

This wasn't the first time that this kind of experiment was done on spiders. In 1948, Swiss pharmacologist Peter N. Witt started his research on the effect of drugs on spiders.

The initial motivation for the study was a request from his colleague, zoologist H. M. Peters, to shift the time when garden spiders build their webs between 2 a.m. and 5 a.m., which annoyed Peters, to earlier hours.

Humans have a very advanced nervous system. Coffee, besides stunning your psychic abilities, greatly damages the nervous system. That's what we are, "nervous systems". The damage done on a physical level, is the end result of the initiated damage done on a nervous/astral level. Many people don't see any damages in their physical bodies yet, but chances are they are already damaged in the mind. That's where everything begins, in the mind, whether it is the poison or the remedy. Witt tested spiders with a range of psychoactive drugs, including amphetamine, mescaline, strychnine, LSD, and caffeine, and found that the drugs affect the size and shape of the web rather than the time when it is built.

## S23 TEA IS HARMFUL, WHILE HERBAL BREW IS NOT

We wrongly use the word 'tea' for everything. There is a difference between tea and brew. Tea is made from the twigs of the tea tree, which is an evergreen, indigenous to Eastern Asia. Some of those twig teas are java, English tea, Ceylon, Jasmine and orange pekoe. A brew is made of the fresh or dry cut herbs. The accurate description would be to call it a 'herbal brew'. Teas contain caffeine and theine. Here's something you may not know – **Tea leaves contain more caffeine than coffee beans**. But since people need more coffee to fill up the amount they drink daily, it works up to the same amount of caffeine.

Herbal brews have no caffeine or theine or tannin. They come in many different flavors (sage, mint, lemon balm, chocolate mint etc.). You can even brew the leaves from strawberries, raspberries, peach, *dandelion leaves* and/or roots.

\*The above mentioned, except the dandelion leaves can be brewed fresh. Personally, I dehydrate everything before brewing. But it's your choice, you can decide to dehydrate them or not. I recommend you dehydrate the dandelion leaves. The brew will be bitter if you brew the fresh leaves. Even though you can add honey and lemon if you wish.

Another recommendation I can give you is to drink the brew without honey or any other sweetener. Unless it's from fresh dandelion leaves. $1^{st}$ of all, what's the point of trying to brew herbs (of various flavors) if you change its flavor by adding honey? And secondly, especially if you are fasting, do not use honey in the brew or in the water. There are digestive stages that happen while you fast, if your body is beyond the sugar levels digestion time, if you consume honey, it's like going back in time, you will mess the body's process toward autophagy.

## SALT – THE MUMMIFYING AGENT

In ancient Egypt, they used salt to preserve the mummies. The real sodium (salt) we need is available in the fruit and vegetables, nuts and anything natural fit for human consumption. Yes, fruit is sweet but it also contains small traces of sodium. Celtic salt and Pink Himalayan are ok temporarily, but eventually, they must not be consumed anymore. Just as we think that external water that we drink is 'life', but instead is death (the internal endogenous water is actually life), so we think the same about salt. The real salt is in the fruit and vegetables.

## S24 SUGAR – THE LEGAL DRUG THAT KILLS YOUR BRAIN CELLS

Sugar is the worst legal drug there is, right up there with tobacco and alcohol. Its uncontrolled use can be a major chemical independence.

Janice Keller Phelps & Alan E. Nourse, in their 1986 book *The Hidden Addiction and How to Get Free*, p. 75, write:

"*The people we are describing are addictive people who are indeed addicted to one of the most powerful substances to be found anywhere – the refined sugars. Their addiction to sugar is a real, harmful, highly damaging health problem, just as debilitating as addiction to any other substance. Like any addiction, when their chemical isn't supplied, they suffer identifiable withdrawal symptoms; like any addiction, the process of feeding their physiological hunger with a chemical is destructive to the body; and like any addiction, the point may be reached when supplying the chemical becomes as painful as withdrawing from it. The cycle of chemical independence becomes both entrenched and intolerable"*

## S25 MEAT – THE DEAD FLESH ENSURING YOU REINCARNATE WITH AMNESIA

Any earthly attachment you have, or any killing you've done, directly (if you yourself killed a person or animal) or indirectly (consuming meat killed by someone else) will ensure you come back here without memories, you'll have to restart the same grade. But you are not condemned forever, you can begin anytime to clear up the negative karma by understanding, accepting and forgiving others (people) and yourself for being hurt by them and hurting them (people and animals). Check **S41** on how to escape the reincarnation cycle.

Animals have different consciousness. In simple terms - we were supposed to eat plants/fruit, which is the first step of falling from grace (while 'breatharianism' was our natural state of being). We were never supposed to kill. Thou shalt not kill isn't religious - it's a universal law. It has a negative karmic effect when we kill. Plants grow from the earth. Animals are born like us and walk the earth. There is a difference. In an ideal world - and how it was supposed to be - we eat the fruit, nuts, seeds that would fall from the plants/trees which we could gather. Our digestive systems aren't designed for meat; hence bowel cancer on a mass scale. It putrefies in the intestines because our intestines are so long (you'll read later on about this).

Science aside, trust your heart. Visit a slaughterhouse and feel if your heart hurts/wants to protect the animals/feels deeply for the animal. Pick some apples/strawberries and feel your heart's reaction. Your heart will never lie. The mind will tell you all sorts of tales and excuses to justify your egos desires. And to not experience it yourself is to remain ignorant to reality. Reality holds the answers - not speculations.

We used to be a civilization where we operated on intuition. The moment we began analyzing everything, we began deteriorating as a species. We must think with our heart and feel with our mind and not the opposite. A meat eater would find excuses as to why we are meat eaters, (the same applies to any one that would defend their choices, including vegetarians) the logical mind blocks the feelings. Have you ever looked in the eyes of an animal? Not a cat's or dog's eyes but the eyes of the animal you eat. Look at him/her (alive cow or chicken) and try to feel that animal as if it's you. Would you want to be slaughtered?

I'll have to remind the readers that when I speak of 'veganism' or 'vegetarianism' I speak of raw natural food (fruit, vegetables, nuts, seeds, herbs in their natural form). Unfortunately, the terms 'natural' and 'vegan' have been bastardized. Store shelves are full of dead, harmful and toxic products labeled 'vegan'. Don't fall for marketing terms printed on the label of the products you buy/consume.

## S26 S P E E D LIMIT – REAL OR ILLUSION?

Another legal drug is "speed limit". First of all, people have become obedient and compliant with tyranny, even though lately more people are awakening. When you drive, psychologically the mind likes the bigger number so you will drive at least in what the limit says you should. The speed limits are already dangerous as it is. If the government added 30 more miles per hour as a limit, then people will drive at that speed.

Why doesn't the government add more to the limit? Because they have data about deaths. Not that they care if more people die. But the way it is right now, enough people die to the point that society remains still functional. Meaning functional according to the controllers' preference. But logically, any sane critical thinker person would notice that this society is a mental facility. Who makes the man-made laws? Those who benefit from when you get sick or when you die.

When you go for a driving licence to fill up the forms, at least in the western world, they ask you to fill up the part where it says in case of an accident if you want to give the permission for your organs to be transplanted to another person in need. How do you know if your organs would be given to another one in need? You don't know. Everyone's body is unique. Even if your internal organs are compatible with another person, your memories will be transferred to that person. When they say a certain organ is compatible, that simply means that the other person receiving the organ will live. Sure, he or she will live, but don't you think that person could have nightmares later on?

This is a subject that needs a whole book in itself exposing the nefarious things they do with human lives. But I'm ending this part in saying to not give permission for your internal organs to be transplanted to another person. You will inflict bad karma. You may ask *"But if I die, how can I inflict karma on myself?"* Karma is inflicted when you are alive. When you sign the document giving them permission to use your organs, then you inflicted bad karma the moment you signed. Because your actions (to sign you have to use a pen, meaning you actively took action) will and can destroy someone else's life, even though you have been convinced that what you are doing is for the greater good.

Karma doesn't care that you didn't know. Ignorance can not be an excuse. There is an exception though, if your own biological child [that has not reached the age of reason yet] needs an organ transplant, then any parent should go ahead and give permission. If your child is already an adult, well, I won't say anything, you can decide for yourself.

Regardless of what you read in this book; it is purely my own opinion (from your point of view). You and only you must decide for yourself. It is your life, and if your path is to destroy yourself and others, then that's on you. Destruction can not be a divine path though. Destroying, ignorance, killing, hate etc. is simply absence of light/ intelligence/creation.

Another way where you can inflict (add) bad karma is when you cut the umbilical cord of your child before he/she is born. Definitely never cut the umbilical cord of anyone else's child. I don't see why you would but just in case you are faced with that decision.

Here are a couple of paragraphs from the book *You Are Not A Strawman You Are The Zygote* by Saimir X. Kercanaj.

**Never cut the umbilical cord yourself** (if you are the father). **The doctor entices the father to cut the umbilical cord, tricking you into thinking it is an honor. Don't fall for it. It is a trap. You will inflict bad karma upon yourself if you cut the cord. 1st of all, you shouldn't have the baby in the mainstream hospital anyway. But just in case that you do.**

"When they offer you to cut the cord, refuse. Let the doctor (medical $taff) cut it, they will inflict bad karma on themselves, not you. If you cut the cord is like killing a sentient being, it's like cutting in half someone. You don't want to do that and pay all your life for something that you could have easily avoided"

Knowledge is important, so even if you are not having any more children, at least let others know about this. But do not wait until someone is pregnant to tell them. I highly recommend the book I just mentioned. I have read most of his books.

You may wonder what all these legal drugs or other subjects in this book have to do with awakening the kundalini or raising the dragon within. Everything in life has to do with sexual energy which is creative energy. We are creators, we create daily, consciously and unconsciously. I will briefly mention a few examples of how sex causes people to behave immorally or irresponsibly. Many men smoke to look cool in front of women. Some of them may disagree but their behavior has to do also with what they've watched in movies, such as when men smoke with women or after finishing having sex. The subconscious mind records everything, and anything recorded in the subconscious, will manifest consciously, depending on the situation and the ignorance/intelligence of the person.

Another example is 'flowers', sex drive or love/lust feelings in general will cause men to give women flowers or sweets or diamonds (which are not really rare by the way), or jewelry. So, just for sex/lust men would feed this beast system by poisoning themselves, the others and by losing their minds over women. The same applies for women but much less, as far as giving gifts/presents. What many women do is much worse. They use their bodies to attract men and not their intelligence (personality/character). All these bad or irrational intentions by both genders contribute in them disconnecting from the source; they operate from their lower mind.

The kundalini will not rise when you live at a low vibrational frequency. Even if you mostly live in high frequency, it takes just one little glass of alcohol or sex with no loving intention to lower your frequency.

## S27 HONEY - A MAGICAL DIVINE MEDICINE

There are live enzymes in honey. When in contact with a metal spoon, these enzymes die. The best way to eat honey is with a wooden spoon. Even if you just scoop out one spoon of honey with a metal spoon, the enzymes of the whole jar's content die and not just the amount that you took out with the spoon. We have habits, we forget, so put a sticker or a tape on the lid of the jar and write "Use only a wooden spoon". Also, plastic spoons must not be used either, whether it's about honey or any other food. Microscopic plastic from the spoon will be entering the food, many people use plastic made spoons to stir fry their food or their soup while cooking. A lot of people say for example "I have been eating this or that or drank this or that for years and here I am, alive". Now, My question to you is "What's your purpose in life, to be alive and just exist or to live your life to the fullest?".

 Honey contains a very important substance that helps your brain work better. Honey is one of the rare foods on Earth that alone can sustain human life. Try to avoid any store bought honey that has an expiry date on the package. Real honey should not expire. One teaspoon of honey is enough to sustain human life for 24 hours. Propolis, produced by bees, is one of the most powerful natural antibiotics. Honey has no expiration date. The bodies of great emperors were buried in golden coffins and covered with honey to prevent putrefaction.

The term "honeymoon" comes from the tradition of newlyweds consuming honey for fertility after the wedding. A bee lives less than 40 days, visits at least 1,000 flowers, and produces less than a teaspoon of honey in its lifetime. One of the first coins had a bee symbol on it. If bees disappeared, life would cease to exist, none of us would be able to survive. The foods that we eat need to be pollinated by bees. And I mean the real natural foods that grow in the ground and not the foods made in labs or factories.

A lot of unhealthy foods have their origin in the ground but by the time they end up in your mouth, they have already been heavily processed. One example is wheat. The bread you eat is made out of wheat flour, but to become bread it will be mixed with unfiltered water, table salt (which is not real salt at all), sugar which is one of the many legal drugs/poisons, cheap manufactured yeast and so on. The more the food is processed/tampered with, the less healthy it becomes. The only real food that should be consumed are the ones that have no ingredient list.

Going back to honey, I have seen articles and/or some short videos of some people saying that honey should not be consumed, that honey is bee vomit. 1s of all, online or nowadays you will find all information to have the opposite too, meaning that for every article/information that says a certain food or drink is healthy, there are articles that say they are unhealthy. In the end, it's you that decides, you are the one to criss cross information and make an educated opinion. But in this case we are talking about natural food, where you don't need scientific explanation as to why natural food is healthy. You must use common sense. This is how I think; bees only consume nectar from the flowers, that's the only thing bees consume. To me it does not matter at all if honey comes from bees' mouths or their butts. People are disgusted by certain things because they associate it with themselves. Humans' vomit and/or poop is not the same as those of the bees. I don't think I need to elaborate anymore on this because it is as clear as a day without chemtrails.

**SOME HONEY HEALTH BENEFITS:**

1. Fights Free Radical Damage
2. Combats Harmful Bacteria
3. Calms Sore Throat and Cough
4. Promotes Oral Health
5. Improves Digestive Health
6. Keeps Blood Glucose Levels in Check
7. Helps Fend off Diseases

## S28 EIGHT STEPS DIET – GRADUAL JOURNEY FROM DEATH TO LIFE

I have seen quite a few people who try to take a shortcut in life, pertaining to health. For something, you can take longer steps, but for others gradual steps are needed. I see arguing between people who prefer meat and those who consume live natural foods (fruit, vegetables, herbs, seeds and nuts). Even if you are, let's say 30 years of age, your cells are carrying information from hundreds of years ago such as: taste, smell, and memories from your parents' lifestyle, grandparents and so on. A gradual progress from degeneration to regeneration scale is needed. Below, I wrote the 8 steps. The last steps ties into Breatharianism. Do not overwhelm yourself with knowledge, no matter how true or logical information is, so go one step at a time.

Foods are *mucus forming* and *non-mucus forming*. The mucus forming causes the blood to become toxic and acidic. These kinds of foods are excreted as mucus or they are deposited as pus. Some of these mucous/pus forming foods are: any **animals dead flesh** a.k.a 'meat, (some are bad and some worse, it doesn't matter, they're all bad), **eggs**, which are simply abortions, **fish** (all fish is contaminated, fish is the lower harmful sentient food), **dairy** products (adult humans are the only species to irrationally consume the antibiotics, puss, HGH of another species), dried fruit (dates, prunes, figs, raisins), nuts and cooked vegetables (the taste remains when you cook them, but the nutrients are gone).

Non-mucus forming foods are those who supply the blood with the mineral elements which are required to carry on vital processes. When you supply the blood with non-mucus forming foods, your blood will be rendered alkaline and thus the blood will be able to neutralize acid-toxins and dissolve and eliminate pus and mucus formed by mucus forming foods.

## Step **O N E – BLOODLESS DIET**

This first step requires the elimination of red meats and substituting it with white meat, eggs and fish. It is very important that you go step by step. If you are someone who is a vegetarian (step 3), then the next step for you is step four. So, depending on where you are at the moment, aim for the next step. There is no specific time/duration between steps, for the fact that different people are at a different internal pollution level, and on a different mindset, some are stronger and some are not so strong. Take it easy, better slow and arrive at the destination (full health/immortality), rather than skipping steps and ending up doing more damage (aging/death).

Why eliminate red meat? The red meat contains a big amount of blood. The terror that the animal went through, that low frequency is still in the meat, on top of the pus and antibiotics contained in the meat. The red meats will instantly acidify your blood. **A meat eater person's heart rate, on average, is 72 beats per minute.** That's 14 beats per minute more than that of a vegetarian. There is a finite (only when you fail to achieve physical immortality through the eighth step) numbers of heart beats in one's lifespan. The worse your diet is, the faster the heart beats will be used, which means early death. Living to a 100 is nothing to be proud about, we are supposed to not age and not die either.

A meat eater's heart beats unnecessarily **7,363,440** (over 7 millions) times per year. Mind boggling, isn't it? A meat eater who is not stressed, but is happy (within decaying self-happiness of our current state of humanity, whether someone eats meat or not), can live longer than a vegetarian who is stressed in general. Stress, anxiety, and mental chaos are more harmful than what you eat. A vegetarian who drinks caffeinated coffee daily, is not much different than a meat eater. Caffeine also shaves off **255,000** heart beats per year out of your lifespan. For each cup of coffee you drink, your heart has to beat **700** times more, that's about one hour of your life each day which is taken off from your lifespan, just by drinking only one cup a day. Think before you end up taking pills or having to have surgeries. Pain while alive is bad. When you die, there is no pain. So, think about your present moments, your choices must be from a self-aware state of mind and heart.

"Since the introduction of meat–eating a.k.a 'rotten flesh' to mankind by the Anunnaki (or Archons?), meat always needed to stay in a cool place, fridge/freezer. Why is that? Because in a warm environment, maggots and parasites would grow on them. The parasites are already in the meat, from the moment that the animal was slaughtered. So, by this logical fact alone, tells us that rotten flesh should not be consumed, because the stomach is warm, and the heat of the stomach is a breeding place for an army of maggots and parasites. And if you say that the acids in the stomach kill everything (which is not true), heat awakens the parasites in the meat the moment it enters the mouth". - *Phisiology & Common Sense*

People live in the mind, many so-called studies are designed to confuse people, or to condition them that what they read makes sense. Not everything that makes sense, makes sense. Feel the truth in the heart and not in the stomach or with the taste buds. Vegans are not that far ahead, many vegans/vegetarians are malnourished compared to some happy meat eaters because they are the ones who consume products bought in stores labeled "vegan". Those products are toxic poisons. Either you consume raw natural food from the ground/trees in their original form or not. There is nothing in between. One is life (*until arriving to the true immortality state at step 8, Cosmic diet a.k.a. "breatharianism"*), the other is death.

## Step **T W O – MEATLESS DIET**

In this step, one should consume eggs, dairy products, fish and anything else but not meat. Because I wrote previously that one should not skip steps, doesn't mean you shouldn't skip any. You must also listen to your intuition. If you are on the first step, but the intuition or your higher self is telling you to go straight into the seventh step, then go ahead. What I write are simply guidelines, you don't have to follow them if you have knowledge of yourself. I was a meat eater for many years. All of a sudden, I felt like going straight to the third step and that's what I did, based on what I felt and not based on what I thought. Thinking can deceive us, but feeling/the heart always tells the truth.

There are many articles and information out there which say that vegetables and fruit have pain when we eat them. Fruit and vegetables are put there to be picked up by our hands. That's why we have hands, to grab things. No animal in existence would willingly put their throat on the knife to be slaughtered. Any animal that is killed, needs to be held tight because no animal would want to die, that's why they have legs for, to run away. It is true that plants have consciousness too; everything has consciousness.

If we go by the logic that plants have pain when they are cut down/harvested, then we shouldn't breathe either, since air is also consciousness. I'm only trying to bring some information which will trigger true self-awareness. Everyone is free to do in their life as they please. Is none of my business to change anyone's life path. But the fact that there is suffering, terror and ignorance in this world, guidance is needed to catapult us into a higher state of consciousness.

## Step **T H R E E – VEGETARIAN DIET**

In this step one should eliminate all animal foods, including eggs and fish. Legumes are a must in this step. Substitute white bread for whole wheat bread, white sugar for brown sugar. Celtic or Pink Himalayan salt for table salt. Table salt should have never been consumed in the first place. It is not salt at all but a chemical cocktail. **A vegetarian person's heart rate, on average, is 58 beats per minute**. Which means that a vegetarian can live longer than a meat eater. If a vegetarian lives a shorter lifespan than a meat eater, that's because either they consume animal products (thinking/believing they are vegetarians; since in our modern world, a vegetarian wrongly is labeled as someone who doesn't eat meat but eats meat byproducts and anything else), or their psyche was fractured, they could be very stressful or perhaps their sexual glands were depleted from too much sex, masturbation or orgasms. There are many things to consider.

So I don't have to mention many factors from different angles I will say this; if a meat eater and a vegetarian (in the true sense as in this step), live the exact lifestyle physically (with the only exception that a meat eater consumes meat and everything else, and a vegetarian consumes everything else from step 3 and above, except meat), emotionally, mentally and spiritually, the vegetarian will live much longer. Human physiology-biology/anatomy is a fact and not an opinion. Later on you will read about the biological difference/facts between humans and animals and you will understand the undeniable truth.

Many people think, or they have been conditioned to believe and act that vegetarianism includes eggs and dairy products. That is a fallacy. Look at the ford 'vegetarianism/vegetarian', it contains the clue as to what it means. **Vegeta**tion, meaning plants, vegetables, fruit, and herbs. If you consume eggs and dairy products but not meat, you are simply on a meatless diet/consumption – 'step two'.

## Step **F O U R** – **RAW FOOD DIET**
Only raw vegetables, fruit, nuts and grains are allowed in this step. We have been conditioned to indulge in a big variety of foods. But when we see for example 'this step', we may think that we don't have many choices now. Yes we do. There are many kinds of fruit, vegetables, grain and nuts in the world. How much do you think you'll eat? Human stomach is very small. We are not supposed to eat like a cow which has 4 stomachs. Technically they have one stomach but four compartments.

It is healthier to consume a meal of just one kind, rather than a mixed salad of different kinds of fruit or vegetables. But this is a more refined step within step four. You go ahead and have a salad for lunch and dinner, but for breakfast it is better if you just have a bunch of fruit of the same kind. Breakfast=break the night's fast. When we sleep, that's unconscious fasting.

Many people have trouble in this step, meaning they don't get full with just fruit and vegetables, but this step also contains nuts. Add a good bunch of nuts in the salad and you'll feel full, but never bloated. Raw food cannot make you bloated. From step four and up, one cannot feel bloated because these steps contain food which are natural to the body, and the body assimilates these foods with ease.

## Step **F I V E – RAW VEGETABLE, FRUIT & SEED-NUT DIET**
This step involves the substitution of nuts for grains. Consume everything from the previous step, except that no grains are used. If you wish, you can eliminate the vegetables in this step. Practice each step, enough days or weeks until they become a way of life, when it doesn't feel forced, so then you will transition to the next steps with ease.

## Step **S I X – HYGIENIC DIET**
This is truly where the hygienic diet really begins. The previous steps are more or less unhygienic. The foods in this step are not mucus forming. These foods are only raw fruit and vegetables. By practicing this step, you can overcome every disease, with combinations of fasts of course. You already read who shouldn't fast, so even if you fall in that category, your diseases will be eliminated when you consume only raw fruit and vegetables. Fasting helps overcome any disease in a shorter amount of time. For as long as you are on a diet from steps 1-5, you will always have mucus in you. Many people who are improving their health even by being on steps 1-4, their improvement is simply based on the previous more harmful step. But when you go one step higher, then you'll realize that the previous step you thought was the right step to be truly healthy, was not so. Do you ever feel heavy or bloated by ingesting air?

## Step **S E V E N – FRUIT DIET**
This step is the best hygienic step to follow, until you are ready for the ultimate step (step 8). Fruit has a higher vibration than vegetables. We are energy/frequency and what we consume dictates our frequency. Even though vegetables fall into the hygienic/high frequency category, they are still of a lower frequency than fruit. They are still good of course, but fruit is much better. Vegetables are intended for animals rather than humans. Humans have been conditioned to eat everything such as snakes, frogs, elephants, dogs, cats, insects, even human flesh. In case you didn't know, there is human flesh (solid or in liquid form) in a lot of toxic foods and drinks people buy in stores, and fast foods. Eat nature (raw fruit).

## Step **E I G H T – BREATHARIANISM or COSMIC RAY DIET**
This is the ultimate diet. In this step your body doesn't require any more earthly foods and drinks. What your body needs to be sustained will be obtained by the cosmic radiation alone, where the source of all

life and nutrition is. How do the seeds under the ground germinate? They germinate from the invisible radiation/cosmic rays which the Sun gives off. Likewise, these cosmic rays generate life electricity in the cells of the human body. The previous hygienic diets/steps ensure a little bit longer lifespan, it is only this step which makes it possible to achieve physical immortality (sexual preservation/continence is a must)

Certain beings which have higher knowledge and have practiced it forever, are physically immortal. You can choose to believe this or not. You create your reality (life or death). Once, I had a friend telling me *"Go ahead, eat air and we'll see how that will work out for you"*. My friend was still on the 1st step. If you think about it, every time you are not eating, you are consuming air. Our very own breath is the clue to the eighth step. Just as the fruit and vegetables that we eat are the clue to one of the major healthy steps. Just as anything we eat are clues as to what we consume is life or death. You will never fully produce endogenous water until you practice dry fast/oxygen fasting (this step).

# S29 12 ESSENTIAL MINERALS THAT ARE A MUST FOR BECOMING A COMPLETE BEING

All of us were born deficient of 3 mineral/cell salts because of the 3 months that we were outside of the womb; we missed out on the Sun supplying in abundance our bodies with the remaining 3 cell salts, based on each individual zodiac sign while in the gestation period. "As above so below", that which is above (Sun, ether, planets a.k.a. the luminaries), is also below (the Earth, plant world, our organs and trillion of cells of our bodies).

Each zodiacal sign forms and influences certain parts of the human body. There are different charts out there, regarding cell salts, based on 12 or 13 zodiacal systems. They can be confusing sometimes. Having in mind that our bodies are damaged from all the toxic poisons from foods, drinks, toxic air (in all big cities), beauty products etc., it means that many people are deficient of more than 3 cell salts or the essential minerals. Therefore, I suggest you pretend you are deficient in all 12, and consume in abundance all foods which contain these minerals. I used to follow certain charts, but there is too much information out there that could rob away your present moment. But there is information that can pinpoint with accuracy as to what exactly everyone is deficient of; there is an ocean of information out there which is not always true. Many times, too much knowledge creates more mental havoc.

I know a dozen people who barely consume any of the foods pertaining to Magnesium or Sodium etc. They are frail, they are barely holding on to their life, with a toe on this side, and the rest of their body on the other side of life. All these foods on the next two pages are rich in the essential minerals, and not just the one on the left (for example 'tomato'). Don't neglect the others, just because the food on the left says, "*is found in largest quantity*'. They are all equally important. You don't know (I don't know either) the amount of minerals your body needs with accuracy, none of us know, that's why I recommend you pretend you are deficient in all 12 minerals. Whether you like certain vegetables/fruit (below) or not, your health is more important than your preferences. I never liked celery, and yet,

49

I consume it. If certain foods are not that tasty to you, add lemon; lemon overpowers any food taste. Don't allow yourself to regret your choices on your deathbed. Refuse to believe that death is normal.

| MAGNESIUM is found in largest quantities in **Tomatoes** | **Magnesium**, which is found in the lungs, brain, muscles & bones, can be found in lettuce, spinach, dandelion, dill but also in cabbage. While calcium is needed for the formation of the bones, it is magnesium that gives them the needed hardness. |
|---|---|
| CALCIUM is found in largest quantities in **Cabbage** | **Calcium** is essential for the formation of the teeth and bones, formation of red blood corpuscles, respiration, & for the beating of the heart. Calcium is found in rich quantities also in spinach, dandelion, dill, lettuce, oranges, lemons and turnips. |
| SODIUM is found in greatest quantities in **Celery** | **Sodium** is essential for the neutralization of carbonic acid in the lungs, formation of the saliva, conduction of electrochemical currents in blood and lymph; it is found in radishes, spinach, asparagus, tomatoes, lettuce, leeks, apples, figs, carrots, swiss chards. |
| POTASSIUM is found in largest quantity in **Tomatoes** | **Potassium** is required by the liver (for glycogen formation), muscles, brain and red blood corpuscles. It is found in high concentration in all fruit and vegetables. Beside tomatoes, next in richness of potassium are, rhubarb, celery and kale. |
| IRON is found in largest quantity in **Lettuce** | **Iron**, as an integral part of the hemoglobin of the red blood corpuscles, it is essential for respiration and oxidation. The next largest in Iron concentration, we have spinach, strawberries, leeks, onions, radishes, celery, carrots, tomatoes, grapes, cherries, cucumbers. |
| MANGANESE is found in largest quantity in **Lettuce** | **Manganese** is contained in the red blood corpuscles. This mineral is found together with IRON. It has similar functions. Therefore, iron is found in largest quantity in Lettuce just like IRON. Consume all the foods in the above table. |

| PHOSPHORUS is found in largest quantity in Kale | Phosphorus is an essential mineral for the function of the brain and the nervous system, muscular tissue of the bones & seminal fluid. Foods rich in phosphorus are: cucumbers, watercress, cauliflower, radish (large), brussel sprouts, sorrel, pumpkins. |
|---|---|
| SULPHUR is found in largest quantity in Kale | Sulphur is essential part of the hemoglobin of the protein of all tissues & all the sulphuric acid salts which have an antiseptic influence in the alimentary canal. Foods in large quantities in sulphur are: Brussel sprouts, cabbage, cauliflower, watercress, dill. |
| CHLORINE is found in largest quantity in Tomatoes | Chlorine is an crucial ingredient of the hydrochloric acid of the stomach and the sodium chloride of the blood. Beside tomatoes, other foods which Chlorine is found in abundance are: Lettuce, kale, dill, celery, radishes, parsnips, spinach, cabbage and carrots. |
| SILICON is found in largest quantity in Lettuce | Silicon is found in nails, muscular tissues, hair (is this the clue for reversing gray hair and baldness?), and pancreas (as silicic acid). Lettuce is the most abundant in silicon. Other foods rich in this essential mineral are: Parsnips, onions, spinach, cucumbers and dandelions. |
| IODINE is found in largest quantity in Sea plants | Iodine is an important mineral for the production of tyrosine/thyroxine by the thyroid glands. Most people who take thyroid medications for life, must know that consuming pineapples, garlic, beets, leeks and red onions will supply them with abundance of iodine. |
| FLUORINE is found in largest quantity in Herbal brew | Fluorine is an important element/constituent of the enamel of the teeth and the iris of the eye. Food that contain fluorine are: grapes, spinach, tomatoes, carrots, oranges, asparagus, beets, prunes, peaches, celery, onions, tomatoes, avocadoes, melons, apples. |

Speaking of fluorine, online, there are a lot of articles saying that fluoride is good for your teeth. That is 100% false. Toothpastes contain synthetic fluorine/fluoride which even if they help your teeth, they would damage your nervous system, the blood, the brain (as we have seen for decades) etc. The same applies to medications/pills, they contain the basic natural chemical, it's that by the time that it is formed into a pill, the end product has become a toxic chemical cocktail. Even if (a big IF) medication/pill corporations had a good intention, to heal people, they could never heal them with processed medications. The only real and truly healthy minerals/cell salts one could consume/take, is from fruit, vegetables, nuts, seeds, and herbs, until one is ready for the eighth step (COSMIC RAYS DIET or BREATHARIANISM), which you read in the previous chapter.

Also, under the 'Fluorine' table/mineral, I wrote 'herbal brew' and not 'herbal tea'. We mistakenly call all brews "teas". As I explained in this book, tea derives from tea trees from Asia. The only so-called "tea" which should be called 'brew' that is free of caffeine/theine are the herbal plants such as: sage, mint, chocolate mint, rosemary, etc. Anything you brew from natural herbs, including leaves from strawberries, raspberries, peach leaves etc., must be called 'brew' and not 'tea'

In each table, I mentioned a few fruits or vegetables. I never mentioned many other fruits and vegetables. Know that all fruit and vegetables or herbs contain these minerals/cell salts, some to a lower and others to a higher quantity/degree.

A natural product (or its elements/minerals) deriving from fruit, vegetables, nuts or herbs cannot be patented. You can't patent nature. That's why all the mainstream medications have been severely changed from their original raw and natural form through extensive processes in the experimental/medical labs. This way, they can be patented. But they are toxic to the human body, they are not fit for human consumption.

Read thoroughly about the important function of each of the twelve minerals they have on the body. Eating a salad a day, or buying organic products without understanding the function of the minerals, won't get us far. As an example, if you lack sodium (salt purchased in stores are not assimilable by the body), not enough saliva will be produced, saliva contains the enzymes to break down the food you eat. With not enough or deficient enzymes saliva, your stomach will be damaged. A lot of people have problems with their stomach, they go to the mainstream doctors (actually mainstream/legal drug dealer), and they get prescribed toxic pills for their stomach, without the root cause being addressed.

Even if you don't have knowledge about health, just by avoiding mainstream doctors/hospitals (with the exception of an accident where you need immediate attention/surgery), you will live longer by default. Women must consume more fruit and vegetables containing iron, especially when they have their period, since the ejection of the blood will waste essential iron needed for optimal health. If you purchase these 12 minerals/cell salt in pill, powder or liquid form, you'll waste your money and cause more damage by adding lab-made products into the body. I will reiterate that only the minerals contained in fruit and vegetables are assimilable by your body, anything else will be rejected.

Sometimes, some people will feel better temporarily, after they take medications. That happens for two reasons:

1) Because of the placebo effect, where if you believe that something can heal you, you will be healed and feel better. In the case of medications/pills, your belief made you feel better and not the pills. But the toxicity in the medications will harm you even further in the long run.

2) When you ingest any toxic pills (all pills are toxic), the toxicity of it, is much higher than the toxicity of your internal body, therefore, the body will prioritize the rejection of the toxicity from the pills, therefore it will stop or minimize the symptoms of whatever (sickness) it is that the body has. Do you get how intelligent our bodies are?

The same applies for when someone takes pain medication. The pain sensors are designed to save you. If you didn't have any pain (sensors) in the stomach, heart or anywhere else, you would die from internal bleeding because you would have failed to do something about it before the point of no return. But of course, there are exceptions, such as if you had a surgery, pain medications are needed. But this need is within this system's heartless function. There wouldn't be any pain (with the exception of accidents) if the system taught people how to live healthy by consuming only raw natural food, exercise, how to think for ourselves, how to reconnect with nature and how to heal ourselves with the power of the mind or any other healing methods such as sound healing therapy, certain other frequency healing techniques etc.

*"Although the organic salts constitute only a comparatively small amount of the body, about 5%, they hold, nevertheless, the key to nearly all of the material manifestations of life; they are the builders of sound*

*and normal cells and tissues, giving them firmness and form. They are conveyors of vital electricity and magnetism, constantly recharging the human dynamo. They are carriers of life-giving oxygen to all the cells of the body, removing at the same time the products of oxidation. They are essential factors in digestion and assimilation and important ingredients of the digestive juices, regulating the osmotic exchange between lymph and blood and cells. In short, they are indispensable for the proper functioning of all the organs and glands, as well as of the nervous system".*
- Otto Carque in his **"Natural Foods"**

If you are someone who ejaculates regularly, you must consume a lot of the foods under 'Phosphorus'. Loss of phosphorus lowers IQ. (Intelligent Quotient). Don't get confused with Intellectual Quotient. One can be very smart intellectually but not intelligent. Intelligence is a balance between both the heart and the brain. True intelligence is when you think with your heart and feel with the brain. If you think with your brain and feel with your heart is intelligence nonetheless, but unfortunately, the majority of people live in the mind, their heart is on vacation, or too much emotional chaos in them.

But even if you are a woman, you too, must consume a lot of phosphorus containing fruit and vegetables. So that I don't have to make examples and explain about each mineral, we (women and men) need to regularly consume all 12 minerals. But we must focus more, at certain times, on a specific mineral, when we feel/know there is something wrong with a specific part of the body. There are many factors to consider in health; food is not the only important thing. Breathing properly (with the diaphragms, neither short nor irregular breaths), thinking positively, meditating, taking sun baths, listening to music at a certain healing frequencies, definitely practicing continence etc. But, usually, food is the main culprit that damages people, because we are not even supposed to eat in the first place.

Animals can be classified, according to their eating habits, into four major groups;

| Frugivorous | Monkeys, apes, bonobos, lemurs, tapirs, chimpanzee. |
|---|---|
| Herbivorous | Cattle, horse, koalas, hippos, pandas, rabbits. |
| Omnivorous | Black bear, pigs, baboons, maned wolves, wild boars. |
| Carnivorous | Arctic wolves, hyenas, lions, honey badger, cougars. |

Some of the animals above may eat foods that belong to a different category. The categories are decided based on anatomical facts, based on how they are designed by the intelligent Creator/Creation. Cats are carnivorous, but guess what people feed cats with? Many feed them cheese, milk and other foods created by man in the factories/labs. In some tourist places, monkeys are fed pizzas, cakes, cookies by tourists. Not only that we have destroyed ourselves with the fake toxic and lifeless diet, but we have damaged the whole ecosystem with our habits and arrogance.

Herbivorous range from tiny insects to some of the largest animals on Earth. There are close to 4,000 different species of terrestrial mammals that are considered herbivores.

As is evident from a consideration of the following anatomical facts, man is a frugivorous creature; his natural diet consists of fruits and nuts. This is so for the following reasons:

1- Herbivorous and omnivorous animals have hooves in order to roam around on grassy plains, carnivorous ones have claws to grasp their prey, while frugivorous ones have hands, to pick fruit from the trees.

**2**- Carnivorous animals drink by lapping up water with their tongue, while man and herbivorous animals drink by suction. The tongue of the former is rough, that of the latter is smooth.

**3**- Carnivorous animals sleep by day, men and herbivorous ones sleep by night.

**4**- The teeth of carnivorous animals have five times the hardness of the teeth of man and frugivorous animals. The former have slightly developed incisors and pointed molars, while the latter have well developed incisors and blunt molars, The argument that man is naturally carnivorous, or omnivorous, because of his "canine" teeth is fallacious, for these eye-teeth are much longer in the frugivorous ape which uses them to crack nuts.

**5**- According to Huxley's classification of animals, by the type of placenta, man is frugivorous. The placenta of the carnivorous animal is of the zonary type; that of omnivorous and herbivorous animals is of the non-deciduate type; while that of man and frugivorous animals is of the discoidal type.

**6**- While all other animals are four-footed, the higher ape and man have two hands and two feet, with flat nails instead of claws or hooves. The former look from side to side as they crawl, the latter look straight ahead as they walk. The former have tails and mammary glands on the abdomen, the latter are without tails, and have mammary glands only on the breasts.

**7**- The alimentary canal of the carnivorous animal is three times the length of its trunk, it is smooth and non-sacculated so that its putrescible contents may be quickly assimilated and eliminated. That of the ape and man, however, is twelve times the length of the trunk, being lined with sacculated valvular folds, so that its frugivorous contents may be retained for a relatively longer period.

**8**- The stomach of carnivorous animals is a simple sac, that of herbivorous animals has three or four compartments; while that of frugivorous ones has a duodenum, or a small second stomach.

**9**- The appendix of carnivorous animals is very small, that of herbivorous animals is larger, that of frugivorous ones is still larger, and that of man is largest of all.

**10**- Carnivorous animals have atrophied sweat glands and have no pores on the skin, Herbivorous and frugivorous animals do have pores and functional sweat glands.

**11**- The salivary glands of carnivorous animals are very small and produce acid secretion which has little effect upon starch, those of man and frugivorous animals on the other hand, are well developed, and produce an alkaline secretion which does affect starch.

**12**- The gastric juice of carnivorous animals has a decomposing and antiseptic influence upon meat, while that of man is far too weak to disintegrate its tough fibers.

**13**- The liver of carnivorous animals is much larger than that of man and frugivorous animals, and is able to destroy proportionately ten to fifteen times as much uric acid.

Disagreeing with the above 13 points is not any different than disagreeing if someone told you that we have 10 fingers in total (unless someone who lost one of their fingers in an accident disagrees). The 'fingers' example is so blatant that anyone would agree, but the internal organs of all animals and humans are created the way they are created to perfection for their intended purpose. But because we have become lazy and conditioned to consume anything that is not in accordance with biology and nature, we dismiss, deny or ridicule anyone who threatens our beliefs. Either we know or we don't. There is nothing in between, as far as biology goes.

Rarely do you see truly balanced people in our current world. There are two major groups of unbalanced people, those who live in the mind, who operate in an intellectual mindset, and those who are good hearted but too naïve, lazy or passive, where they expect solution or salvation from imaginary external deities/figures.

Often we hear that humans have been eating meat since ancient times. What is "ancient times" 500 years ago, 1000 years ago, 10,000 years ago? People have been eating meat since THEY (Anunnaki/Archons?) introduced it to people. People waste too much time debating or arguing about politics, sports, flat/globe earth, carnivorism/veganism etc. and it's how they control mankind, by pinning people against each other.

By having read the **8 steps from death to life**, the **12 essential minerals** and this chapter, if you take a step back and analyze yourself, your current life, the world and your past life choices, you should have a wider perspective on creation, and you will know (not think or believe) what's the right thing to do, based on the universal laws (not man-made laws).

It is your life, you can do with your life as you please. If you obey the natural laws, you will not age, nor die. If you infringe the natural laws, you will continue to degenerate biologically, mentally and spiritually and you will certainly die. There is no doubt about that, we are not above the laws that created us and everything in the creation.

Five thousand years into the future, that generation will see us as their ancestors. Do you think they should believe and follow in our footsteps? We haven't learned to take care of each other yet. We fight over lands, imaginary gods, materialistic false gods. We are an arrogant and selfish species, we abuse ourselves and others, the animals and nature. How could we be an example for the future generations?

Seeds such as: pumpkin, pine kernels, sunflower, sesame etc., are the best substitutes for animal proteins. Animals take their proteins from what grows on the ground (speaking of the animals raised only with raw natural food and not the thousands plus toxic foods created by the meat industry). Don't you think it's best to consume the proteins straight from the seeds which are in their most raw and natural state?

# PART TWO
## THE POISON OR THE REMEDY

# M I N D

"The only true wisdom is in knowing you know nothing  – **Socrates**

"For a man to conquer himself is the first and noblest of all victories"– **Plato**

"You have power over your mind, not outside events. Realize this, and you will find strength"
– **Marcus Aurelius**

Generally, we have become a lazy species. We may not be lazy about certain things but lazy about others. I had a $35 credit balance from my last cellphone provider since 2018. Six years, times 12=72. A lot of trees were cut down unnecessarily to make paper for the mail sent every month since 2018. 72 times going by the road to pick up the mail, 72 more potential dangers being hit by cars driving by. All this just because I was too lazy to take care of it. I took care of it just by a phone call.

> **"Laziness may appear attractive, but work gives satisfaction"**
> - Anne Frank

By "work gives satisfaction", Anne means to engage with passion in anything that we do, and not work as in working for someone to earn a paycheck. I have seen countless people, adults, especially younger people, in their 20s, where they feel bored and are too lazy to even do basic operations as a human being.

Some of them don't do their bed, when they finish a package of juice, they're too lazy to throw it out. If they finish the content of a package from the fridge, they put it back in the fridge empty. Too lazy to change the toilet paper. After they are done showering (I'm surprised they even shower, I would think they were allergic to water), the floor is messy with their clothes, towels etc. If for whatever reason a shirt or something else is on the floor, they walk over it, they don't even pick it up. I could mention countless examples, but I think it is enough, I'm sure you'd have to have witnessed similar situations. The situations I mentioned are from people I know.

This whole generation (there are exceptions of course) has become too lazy, and one of the reasons is that children nowadays have so many things in the house, so many devices that they waste too much time on them. And when they don't use said devices, they are too lazy to clean the house or fix something that needs fixing, because their brain is wired to their new environment (porn, movies, sports, videogames). It takes just a few days to interact with the same thing, and you will be entangled in it.

It applies the same thing to the opposite. If you practice for a few days (and continue the practice) meditation, conscious breathing, engaging with nature, listening to healing music, practicing some form of crafting/artistry, then you will be entangled with these, and your soul will be filled with joy.

Be the King or the Queen of your temple, where you have dominion over your kingdom. Back in the day, when Kings and Queens existed (some do still exist now), they had dominion over the people, that was a tyrannical rulership. Tyranny/rulership exists only because ignorance exists, which brings laziness. When you harmonize your thoughts, words and actions, then your inner dominion can only be controlled by you. Suffering, in most people exists because of internal conflict between the thoughts and emotions. When thoughts and emotions become harmonized, conflict will be a thing of the past.

## S32 MEDITATION IS NOT EVIL. THE CONTROLLERS WANT YOU TO THINK SO

Certain religions (beLIEf systems/ideologies) teach that yoga and/or meditation are demonic and satanic. The reason they teach that is because of what happened hundreds of years ago. When Britain invaded India, they had trouble controlling the population, who were very in tune with their bodies. Due to dedicated ancient yoga and meditation practices, many Indians had developed 'Siddhis' (special abilities unexplained by modern science. Some of those abilities were: telekinesis, psychic and shamanic powers, levitation etc). This is why the controlling system had the church teach that yoga and meditation were evil. They wanted to stop others from developing these innate human abilities, which threaten their control.

This happens to some extent with ALL religions. Group consciousness, or in this case hive mind mentality follows specific predictable patterns. Not a case of good or bad but part of the natural process on the way to self realization. The path to self-realization exists, whether one realizes and walks the path through hard trials or through conscious self-aware thinking.

Our physical eyes can only see a small bandwidth of light/information. When you meditate you can see beyond the confines of the physical eyes. A lot of people meditate but many of them just do it as an activity without delving deeper within themselves and the worlds beyond. You can meditate any time of the day if you wish, but it's best when your mind is relaxed or else, thoughts won't stop bothering you. You can use meditation music if you wish, until you are ready to meditate in complete silence. One main reason for all the suffering in our world is because we live in the mind, meaning "conscious mind". We overanalyze everything, which then we become frequently emotional. Nobody else but you are the one responsible to bring yourself in a peaceful state.

Meditation helps with stress in the moment, but regular practice can actually change your brain. Harvard neuroscientist Sara Lazar, PhD, did a study to determine if meditation increases gray matter in the brain. And then, just to be sure, she did a second study. Results showed that just eight weeks of daily meditation can change the brain to process stress differently, leading to decreased anxiety and depression and an overall increase in quality of life. I can attest to this myself.

"Minds are busy all the time," says Nina Smiley, PhD, director of mindfulness programming at Mohonk Mountain House and co-author of *The Three Minute Meditator* and *Mindfulness in Nature*. "Minds are constantly thinking, planning, perceiving beauty and figuring things out, and having a mind that's constantly in motion can be exhausting. It can be stressful. Meditation is a skill that helps us begin to work with the mind as we learn to be present in a different way, bringing calmness and clarity into the moment, whatever it may be."

## S33 PRANAYAMA – BREATHING MEDITATION TECHNIQUE

While we often simplify the term pranayama to mean "breathwork," the yogic meaning of pranayama is more nuanced. In Sanskrit, "prana" means "life force," and describes the energy that is believed to sustain the life of the body. "Ayama" translates as "to extend, expand, or draw out," although some say that the word is actually derived from "yama," meaning "control."

In her book *Yoga: Ancient Heritage, Tomorrow's Vision*, **Indu Arora** breaks it down even further. "Pra means 'primary, first, innate.' Ana, from anu, means 'the tiniest, smallest, indestructible unit of energy,'" according to Arora.

With either translation, you arrive at the same concept: Pranayama is a practice that involves the management or control of the breath. As implied by the literal translation of the term, yogis believe that this practice not only rejuvenates the body but actually extends life itself. Pranayama consists of different breathwork techniques designed to gain mastery over the respiratory process while recognizing the connection among breath, mind, and emotions.

There are many techniques but one basic one is the "Diaphragmatic Breathing"

The diaphragm is the primary muscle that controls breathing. It's a large dome-shaped muscle located between lungs and your belly, just below the ribcage. it moves up and down when you breathe, allowing air to pass through into your lungs. The intercostal muscles between ribs are considered separate accessory breathing muscles. These are activated during chest breathing and require more effort and energy than using the diaphragm.

Here, you can test and learn how to breathe with your diaphragm like this:

**1)** Lie on your back on a flat surface or bed, with your knees bent and your head supported. Use a pillow under your knees to support your legs.

**2)** Place one hand just below your rib cage and the other on your upper chest. This will allow you to feel your diaphragm move as you breathe.

**3)** Breathe in slowly through your nose so that your stomach moves out, causing your hand to rise. The hand on your chest should remain still. If the hand on your chest moves, then you are not doing it right.

**4)** As you begin to exhale, tighten your stomach muscles, so that your stomach moves in, causing your hand to lower. The hand on your upper chest should remain as still as possible.

Practice this for a few minutes a day until you can breathe with your diaphragm even when you walk, without having to put your hands on your chest or belly. Eventually, you will be in control of your breathing, and you will feel the stomach going in and out while inhaling/exhaling.

You can practice this (5-steps) easy pranayama technique for 5-10 minutes 1-2 times per day.

**Step 1** – Sit in a stable and comfortable position with your spine straight and long. If seated on the floor, you can use a cushion or folded blanket under the back of the hips for support. If seated on a chair, make sure both feet are flat on the floor.

**Step 2** – Close your eyes or soften your gaze and take several deep breaths through your nose. Allow your body to relax and bring your awareness to your breath. Make sure there is no tension in the shoulders, neck or face.

**Step 3** – Put a hand on your upper chest and a hand on your stomach. Inhale slowly through your nose until you feel your stomach rise slightly against your hand. Exhale slowly and feel your stomach fall away from your hand towards your spine.

**Step 4** – Work towards having your breaths be slow and deep with only the stomach moving. Try to keep the chest as still as possible. Continue with these deep breaths for several minutes.

**Step 5** – Once you have learned the technique, work on applying belly breathing during yoga classes while holding poses, or if you practice at home by yourself.

While you meditate, you can listen to healing music if you wish. Personally, I use different varieties to complement my yoga or exercise in general. I listen to healing frequency (111hz, 432hs, 528hz etc.) music, wave/ocean sounds, birds and piano sounds, fire crackling or bee sounds. They are all soothing, but you can choose whichever makes you feel best.

Proper meditation will get you above the conscious mind. Bill Donahue, in one of his seminars, said this about the importance of meditation:

> "He who cannot meditate, must not expect peace, because the object of meditation is to raise yourself above the thoughts of the mind and into the bliss that Carl Jung called "Super Consciousness", into the bliss that Buddha called "Nirvana", into the bliss that Jesus called "The Kingdom of God within you". When you take the human spirit and raise it up into the place where there is no thought (no stain of thought), it becomes the Holy Spirit/the Virgin Consciousness"

Without meditating, peace cannot happen, and without peace, happiness cannot be attained. A lot of emotional chaos happens in the world as a result of a clouded mind. Meditation clears the mind, just as when you let the water be, any dirt or mud, will fall and reside in the bottom. Likewise, if you stop feeding your life with the six thieves (**eyes, ears, nose, tongue, body** and **mind** (lower 'm') – you will read about these thieves later on), all that will be left is, "peace". Peace is like calm water. Bruce Lee said, *"Water can flow or it can crash, be water, my friend"*.

# S34 PINEAL GLAND / THIRD EYE

**Pineal Gland – Facts, Location, Fluoride, Cyst, Calcification and Function.**

The pineal gland is a small organ situated near the center of the brain, whose secretory function is not fully understood yet, or is it?. However, it is actually an important part of your endocrine system.

It is known to be influenced by light, it is connected to the day-night cycle, sleep, and sexual development, yet there is more to learn about it. We barely know anything, even though it seems like we have learned a lot about it. The epiphysis played an important role in one of the greatest thinkers that mankind has ever had – René Descartes. He described it as the place in which all the information is filtered, stored, and processed, and then sent throughout the body.

Moreover, the French philosopher argued that here is where the human soul is found, so that the entire coordination is possible. It is said that the pineal gland is the seat of the soul.

It's called pineal because it has the shape of a pine cone, the size of a pea, weighing about 0.2 g (or much more if it's fluoridated). This

gland is better known as the third eye, Ajna chakra, or the eye of Horus. The pineal gland is able to perceive light, just as the normal eyes do, but it secretes melatonin only in the dark. It is important that you sleep or meditate in total darkness so that the pineal gland secretes adequate melatonin.

The secretion of melatonin is inhibited by light and stimulated by its absence, which is one of the reasons why you should not sleep with the lights on. Make it a habit to not look at your cellphone as soon as you wake up. But if you do, I recommend you use Blue Light Blocker glasses if you have to use electronic devices, including Tv, but also while you are at home when the Sun is down because the led/fluorescent light bulbs you have in the house are harmful. All this technological pollution affects the pineal gland where it won't produce the required melatonin needed for healing the body and the mind.

As melatonin is released and spread throughout the body, we enter into a deeper sleep. Melatonin is known as an anti-stress and anti-aging agent since it both suppresses cortisol and is a strong antioxidant.

**Fluoride**

Inside, the pineal gland is filled with water, which calcifies in time (it becomes visible on radiographs after the age of 20) due to fluoride in toothpaste, fluoride in water or soda. Additionally, sources of fluoride can include processed foods and beverages made with fluoridated water.

Aryana Havah said:

*"Fluoride has no beneficial effect on the body – It is given specifically to inhibit the Pineal Gland."*

The epiphysis may be the location of a very rare tumor, called the pinealoma.

Note – fluoride was first added to toothpaste in 1914, however, it was only in 1955 that the first commercial fluoride toothpaste became available. In 1951, fluoridation became an official policy of the U.S. Public Health Service. According to a recent study, prenatal exposure to higher levels of fluoride increases the incidence of attention-deficit/hyperactivity disorder as well as impairs cognitive development in children. A 2019 draft report from the National Toxicology Program established that fluoride is "presumed" to be a cognitive neurodevelopmental hazard to humans.

Since the gland is not protected by the blood brain barrier, it is open to exposure to minerals like fluoride and calcium. Any cyst or calcification that occurs in the epiphysis shows that there are energy blockages on that level. Also, it can lead to excessive sleepiness or insomnia. Studies conducted by various researchers have shown that such formations – cysts, calcifications – can occur at any age.

**Ways To Decalcify Your Pineal Gland**

LSD

Drugs like LSD or DMT have the ability to open it strained and accelerate its functioning. Dr. Rick Strassman, author of *DMT: The Spirit Molecule*, noticed among other things that the epiphysis produces DMT during birth, death, during spiritual or mystical experiences.

Strassman explained:

*"As an endogenous, or naturally-produced, human psychedelic, I believed it might mediate spontaneous psychedelic experiences such as near-death and mystical states."*

Dr. Rick Strassman went on to say:

*"I also considered the epiphysis a source of this endogenous DMT; as such, the pineal might be a 'spirit gland."*

It is proven that the epiphysis is directly related to sexual function, and sexual abstinence (abstention from excesses) can strongly activate it.

It was noted that the persistence of negative emotions, such as fear, anger, and feelings of denial of one's own being, affects the pineal gland negatively.

Herophilos (335–280 BC), a Greek physician and often called the father of anatomy, noted that the small pineal gland is a single structure, different from the brain's characteristic of mirrored sides: left and right.

It is the first gland to be formed in the fetus, fully formed around the 49th day after conception and is identifiable at 3 weeks. It is also heavily vascularized. The pineal gland is nourished with the best blood, oxygen, and mixture of nutrients from human anatomy, being surpassed only by the kidneys (whose function is to filter impurities from the blood).

Due to these special and unique anatomical configurations, Herophilos correctly concluded that this gland plays a major role in consciousness and that it is the gateway to our real self.

**Symptoms That Your Third Eye Is Opening**

Spiritual Third Eye facts:

There is a direct similarity between the epiphysis and the eyeball, due to the fact that the epiphysis also has crystalline receptors for the perception of colors; the internal structure of the gland is similar to the eye retina; it contains photoreceptor cells called pinealocytes. Therefore, it is called the third eye or spiritual eye.

David Wilcock, the New York Times bestselling author of "*The Source Field Investigations*," said:

"*It is apparent that several relationships exist between the pineal gland and retina. The similarities in development and morphology have been obvious for many years.*"

In Vedic texts, the epiphysis is considered the "third eye" – designed to facilitate communication with the divine power, and self-knowledge. It is also the seat of awareness, the gateway to cosmic realms within, freedom, and discrimination.

"All psychic systems have their physical aspects in the body. With Ajna chakra, the physical equivalent is the pineal gland, which has long baffled doctors and scientists as to its precise function. Yogis, who are scientists of the subtle mind, have always spoken of

telepathy as a 'siddhi', a psychic power for thought communication and clairaudience, etc. The medium of such siddhis is Ajna chakra, and its physical terminus is the epiphysis, which is connected to the brain. It has been stated by great yogis that it is the receptor and sender of the subtle vibrations which carry thoughts and psychic phenomena throughout the cosmos." – Swami Satyananda

## Practices For Pineal Gland Activation

### Acupuncture

The third eye chakra corresponds to the acupuncture point M-HN3, in Chinese medicine. The seed (beej) sound for this chakra is "Eem."

When the third eye functions harmoniously, it confers inner balance, well-being, and a tendency toward spirituality. However, malfunction of epiphysis or even blockages in this area leads to exacerbated attachments to the material world and the fear of death. If someone is afraid of dying, that person doesn't have an opened pineal gland.

Moreover, everything from dizziness and headaches to brain lesions and blindness can be linked with an unhealthy third eye chakra. If you have a blocked Ajna chakra, you might also struggle to learn new things and have trouble sleeping (insomnia). Third eye chakra healing employs different types of holistic healing remedies to bring alignment to the mind, body, and spirit.

### Sungazing – FOOD FOR THE PINEAL GLAND
Sun gaze or Sunbath anytime you see the Sun up. The skies are getting polluted daily with aerosol injections and other toxic substances. But still, the sun's electromagnetism can still penetrate the clouds. With the exception of napping during the day, any other time, for as long as the Sun is up (regardless if it's covered by clouds or not), our eyes/retina should be hit by light. Many people (including me in the past) spend many hours a day watching movies in darkness, which damages the person's biological internal clock.

## S35 STEREOGRAM – SEE 3D IMAGES IN A 2D IMAGE WITH A "CROSS EYE – VIEW" METHOD, WHICH HELPS THE THIRD EYE OPEN

Have you ever been able to see a 3D image within a 2D flat plane/ image? What are 3D stereograms? A stereogram is a plane image or a pair of two-dimensional images that, when appropriately viewed using both eyes, produces an image which appears to be three-dimensional. The three-dimensional effect can be produced by both eyes looking at a single image  by defocusing the eyes at a certain distance. These are called "random-dot stereograms".

MOTHER AND CHILD DOLPHINS
SWIMMING

Initially, I wanted to write what 3D image is hidden in each one of these three 2 dimensional images, but then I changed my mind. I know, this is nothing new to many, but there are still many other people who never knew about this subject. I find stereograms cool.

But the main reason for me putting these images here is for the purpose of helping with the pineal gland.

But then, I changed my mind again and wrote on top of two of the images what is hidden within them. The one above (heart inside a star) is the best, especially if you got the color version of the book. Didn't want some readers to become frustrated. At least you have an idea what you'll find hidden here. Speaking of the pineal gland, by crossing your eyes, it balances both brain hemispheres. Whenever you try this, do it for a few seconds and then uncross back your eyes and try again in 30 seconds or so. Don't defocus/cross your eyes for more than 10 seconds.

Stereograms are intriguing images which can provide insight into the power of human perception and the complex relationship between human brain and eyes. When you defocus enough you will be able to see the hidden images that pop up out of the background or sink into it. In this book the three images I chose have a 3d object (woman, dolphin, butterfly) which pops out of the background. I prefer these more than the ones which sink into the background. I find the stereograms delightful experiences. Online, you can find countless stereogram images.

# WOMAN DANCING

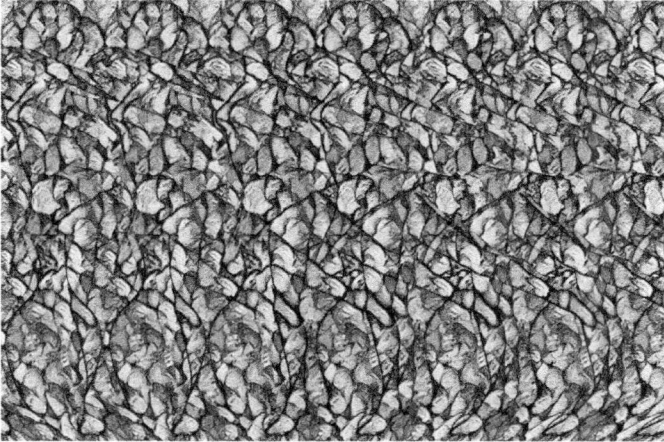

Two techniques on how to reveal/view a 3d object within a two-dimensional flat plane/image.

**Techniques for Viewing Stereograms**
Viewing stereograms can be a fascinating experience, but it requires certain techniques to properly perceive the **hidden 3D images**. Here are two well-known methods to help you **see stereograms**: the Relaxing View Method and the Diverging View Method. (check also the wiki article at the end of this chapter, which explains with pictures on how to view stereogram images.)

**The Relaxing View Method**
The Relaxing View Method, also known as the Parallel View Method, is one of the easier techniques for beginners trying to see the hidden images in stereograms. This method involves looking 'through' the image as if gazing into the distance.

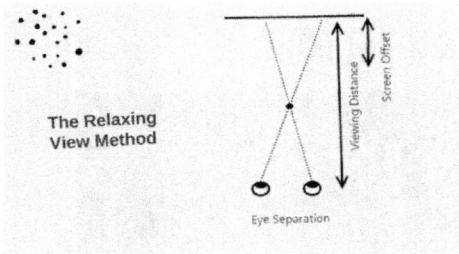

The Relaxing
View Method

1. Hold the stereogram close to your face, touching your nose, and slowly pull it away while keeping your eyes relaxed.

2. Direct your gaze as if you are looking through the image into the distance. Your focus should be beyond the plane of the image.

3. The hidden image will start to come into view as a 3D object. It may take several attempts to bring the image into focus.

4. Once you see the 3D image, hold your focus. If you lose it, bring the image back to your nose and repeat the steps.

It is essential to maintain a relaxed gaze and avoid the urge to focus directly on the surface of the picture.

**The Diverging View Method**
The Diverging View Method, also known as the Cross-Eyed Method, might be more challenging for some but can be effective in viewing stereograms.

**The Diverging
View Method**

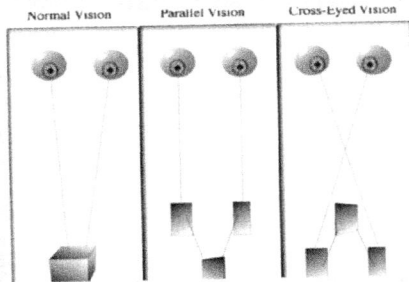

1. Hold the stereogram at a comfortable distance in front of you.

2. Cross your eyes slightly and focus on a point between you and the image. You should see two overlapping images.

3. Adjust the level of divergence until the two images align to form a third image in the center.

4. The central image will appear to be in 3D. Try to keep your eyes crossed while looking at this image to maintain the 3D effect.

This technique may require more practice and can be more straining on the eyes. If you find this method difficult, consider trying the Relaxing View Method or reading more about magic eye stereograms for alternative approaches.

Both these methods involve training your eyes to see things differently, and with patience and practice, you can master the art of viewing stereograms. For those interested in creating stereograms themselves, understanding these techniques is also beneficial. If you're curious about how stereograms trick the brain into seeing 3D images, you can learn more by reading auto stereograms explained.

**Tips on How to See Stereograms Successfully**
Unlocking the secrets of stereograms can be a rewarding experience,

but it requires the right approach. Here are some tips for mastering the art of viewing these hidden 3D images.

**Creating the Right Environment**
To maximize your chances of success, it's crucial to view stereograms in an environment conducive to concentration and relaxation. Here are factors to consider when preparing your setting:

- **Lighting:** Ensure the room is well-lit but without direct glare on the stereogram.

- **Position:** Hold the stereogram at eye level, or position it on a flat surface with no distractions in the background.

- **Distance:** Start close to the image and gradually move it away from your face as you attempt to focus.

A calm and comfortable setting will help your eyes relax, making it easier to adjust your vision to see the hidden 3D images within stereograms.

**Eye Exercises to Improve Focus**
Improving your focus can be beneficial when trying to view stereograms. Here are simple exercises to enhance your eye coordination and focusing ability:

**Near and Far Focus:**
- Find a point close to you and another one farther away.
- Shift your focus back and forth between these two points for a few minutes.

**Figure Eight Tracing:**
- Imagine a horizontal figure eight a few feet in front of you.
- Trace the figure with your eyes slowly.

**Palming:**
- Rub your hands together to generate warmth.

- Gently place your palms over your closed eyes without pressing.
- Relax and breathe deeply for a few minutes.

These exercises can help prepare your eyes for the unique demands of viewing magic eye stereograms.

**Patience and Practice**
Mastering the skill of seeing stereograms doesn't happen overnight. It requires patience and consistent practice. In my case, it took me a few tries within minutes to successfully be able to view the hidden 3D images. Many times when I was younger, I was crossing my eyes, as a fun game with friends. Maybe that's why I was able to view the stereograms with ease, or not.

Here are some strategies to enhance your learning curve:

- **Daily Practice:** Dedicate a few minutes each day to practice viewing stereograms.

- **Record Progress:** Keep a log of your attempts and successes to track improvement.

- **Variety:** Experiment with different types of stereograms to challenge your perception.

Remember, the key is to be patient with yourself. Each attempt brings you closer to experiencing the wonder of auto stereograms explained in full 3D.

**Common Challenges and Solutions**
Mastering the art of viewing stereograms can be a rewarding experience, but it often comes with its set of challenges. Understanding these common hurdles and how to overcome them is key to unlocking the hidden 3D images in stereograms.

**Difficulty in Focusing**
One of the most common issues people encounter when learning how to see stereograms is difficulty focusing on the image in the correct way. The trick is to look through the image, not directly at it. This can be counterintuitive, as we're accustomed to focusing on the surface of an object to see it clearly.

**Eye Strain and Fatigue**
Staring at a stereogram for prolonged periods can lead to eye strain and fatigue. This is especially true for beginners who are not yet accustomed to the techniques required to view these images. To prevent discomfort, it's important to take regular breaks and not strain the eyes excessively.

I use the 2$^{nd}$ technique. I can immediately see the hidden object in any stereogram image. It is because years ago I was into these delightful experiences and I was looking at a lot of these kinds of images. Anyone is capable of properly seeing 3D stereogram images. But I just tried technique number one and I can immediately see the hidden images.

If you are interested to read about the science behind stereograms, you can check the articles below, or any other article. A quick search online will give you the results you desire.

**https://www.wikihow.com/View-Stereograms**
**https://eyefitness.fit/how-to-see-stereograms/**

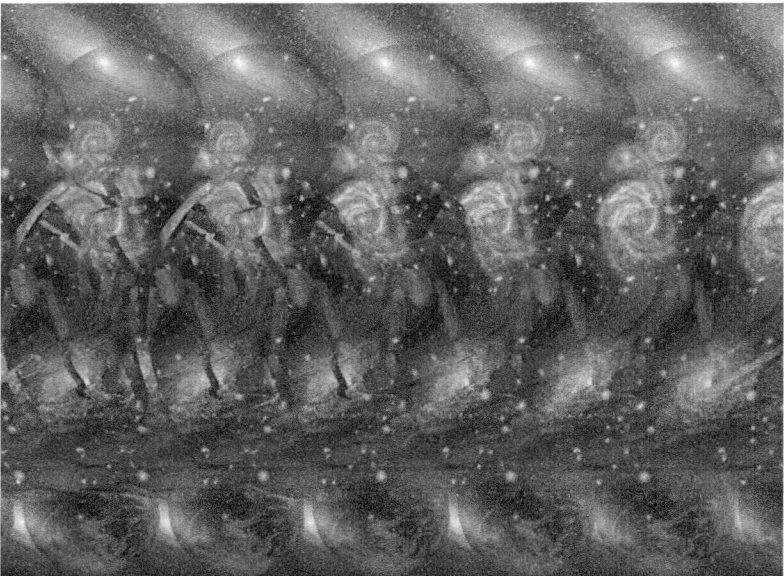

While looking at the hidden 3D object, move your head away from the book, it should become an even clearer image, but not 5

kilometers away; you decide.

# S36 RELIGION – SCIENCE - PHILOSOPHY

Why make a conflict of these, when you can apply and use all 3? Religion (not the organized one) shows who and how philosophy tries to understand the wisdom coming from God. Science observes God's laws. By "God" I don't mean an actual physical person.

Being spiritual and having an open belief system will allow you to accept all three. As new research comes in, you can change your beliefs. You hear something you like; you can incorporate it into your belief system, and you can do your own research as you please. All three include bits of each other, philosophy explains life lessons from religion. Science theories require faith. Religion needs observation and further studying. Every main religion has been corrupted. But the main messages stand. You can't have one without the others. Science wouldn't exist without religion, philosophy wouldn't either as it was used to argue against Greek mythology etc.

The question is how has each one helps in human development and well being and welfare of humanity and environment? All three are hijacked, and also people who rely blindly on all three are also hijacked to the point that any of the three groups of people argues with the other two, in defending their beliefs, rationality or observation.

Philosophy is based on subjugation to wisdom (the ability to make good decisions). Science is a branch of philosophy for generating knowledge about the quantity of the world so as to be able to make good decisions. Spirituality, like science, is also a branch of philosophy, although instead of investigating the quantity of existence spirituality seeks to investigate the quality (meaning, what is "good") of existence.

> **Many religious people's heart is in the right place, but their mind is not rational, in the context of the divine existence with everything in it.**

Religion (organized religion) is based on human subjugation, the subjugation of humans to a system of control that benefits a small group of "leaders". This subjugation works by the "religion" defining what is "good", referencing the concept of quality to a concept of "God" that is wholly created by the humans who developed the religion and is unable to be verified through philosophic or scientific means (you have to have "faith" - not in God itself, but in the humans who are describing God to you).

Humans are falling back into a "dark age" or so it seems, where beliefs and fantasy are more important than reality. The antidote to this dark slide is found through uniting the three aspects of human knowledge, philosophy, science, and spirituality, for good. We are able to define a universal measure of quality, a concept of what is "good" based on our understanding of the order inherent to this universal existence as illuminated through our exploration with modern science and philosophy.

Many scientists' intention is genuine but their beliefs in only what they can physically see, jeopardizes their ability to feel, rationally analyze from a broader horizon point of view and their ability to sense the unseen, is put on the back seat. We rationalize or philosophize, and yet, our thoughts cannot be seen, until they have become actions. Our feelings can cause us to rationalize (in a healthy or unhealthy way) and then act responsibly or irresponsibly, which will then be manifested in the physical reality.

The greatest philosophical work of our age, possibly of the last few hundred years, is a perspective of universal evolution (the evolution of systems) that shows there is an underlying order to our universe which we are able to use to functionally define an objective morality (a universal measure of quality).

All three try to reach the ungraspable of our minds. We are limited in all 3 when we lean more toward one than the other two. The truth is scattered everywhere, each of the 3 contains one piece of the puzzle. When science, religion and philosophy work together for the betterment of mankind without personal gain and without ego tendencies, will then mankind see peace.

People argue or hold on tight only to the branch they like or feel the most, but we must broaden our horizons; we must allow ourselves to consider that the true reality is a whole puzzle, where our reality is only a small piece of the puzzle.

All three are needed. All three (religion, science, philosophy) are hijacked by those who want us to fight among each other. You cannot live in peace if you are missing one of the three. My logic here is based on knowing and accepting that the unseen (astral realm, the quantum field or God, feelings and thoughts), and what we see (the physical world and ourselves) are both sides of the same coin.

Many philosopher's (whether they are/were famous people or regular people like you and me who lean/leaned toward philosophy) logic is/was valid, but their heart and intuition was/is suppressed.

Many people argue, or like/dislike others based on their zodiac sign. But what they don't know or perhaps they do but don't want to admit or accept, is that we are all signs. Each zodiac sign influences different parts of the body. If you take out one of the constellations, every single being will instantly die/disintegrate. The same way people argue over religion, philosophy or science. We are all three. We have a body (SCIENCE), a heart (RELIGION) and a brain/mind (PHILOSOPHY).

Take out one of these and you are dead. Not literally but like a walking dead. I must remind you that this explanation is based on accepting all three from an open heart and a rational mind. To live in peace and harmony, one must harmonize both the heart and the mind, otherwise, one will be living like an invalid. Disease is not just physical, it can also be mental or spiritual. Many people who are physically invalids, are intelligent and have a good heart, while others who have no physical problems are apathetic and/or naïve. Which one is better?

## S37 EMOTIONAL POLLUTION

One way to emotionally pollute yourself is to eat readymade food from others, from friends, coworkers and especially from restaurants. The food from the restaurants are the ones who are most exposed to harmful energies which surrounds the foods they make. If the person who cooks the meal for you at a restaurant (fast food places are even worse) is in a low vibrational state, suicidal, negative state, the energy of that person is immediately transferred to the food that they cook for you. You never know in what state these people/workers are.

Most of them smile (being fake) at you because you are a customer, many of them are taught to fake their smile, meanwhile they are suffering inside. Most people hate their jobs. Hate/dislikement is very low vibrational energy. It is much better to cook/prepare your own food. Not only that, but you must also infuse the food you prepare with positive energy. The same way another person can transfer negative energy to the food that you order from, so will you transfer your own negative energy into the food that you prepare for yourself.

Do not cook/eat when you are in a bad mood. Many people when they are stressed they eat, what they don't know is that they infuse the food they eat with death. If you are someone who overeats and is trying to shift into a lighter diet, the best way to make the transition is to practice conscious fasting. Your system has been working nonstop and it needs to rest.

Fasting provides the much-needed rest for your body. When you fast regularly, eventually your stomach will shrink back to its original size. Your appetite will return back to normal. One important thing that you must know is to not overeat after long fasting sessions. I made the mistake of overeating many times. I was (and still am) very strong in resisting without eating for 30, 40 or even 50 hours without food but I failed by overeating when I would break the fast. When you train yourself with conscious fasting, the stimulated nerves will come down. If it is difficult to fast on just water, then begin to fast on juices and smoothies until you are ready to fast on just water.

The emotional pollution makes it difficult to consciously fast for long periods of time. Let alone that you are bombarded visually by food products from social media/ads or the circumstances. When fasting becomes a way of life, all your emotions should be balanced or tamed where you have your emotions under control and not being controlled by them.

## S38 BE A LEADER AND NOT A FOLLOWER

Let me begin by saying that any politician is not a leader but a controller (actually a puppet). Don't waste any more time with them. The more attention you give to something, the more powerful it becomes. Water yourself, give attention to yourself, your actions and your emotional state. Your aim should be to work for yourself, when you do that, life is not anymore a prison; it becomes a school. No matter how good of a position you may have where you work, you are still treated as a slave. If you don't think so, then the chains are longer, and you can't see them. In fact, there are no chains, it is all in the mind.

> **"The best way to keep a prisoner from escaping is to make sure he never knows he is in prison"** - Fyodor Dostoevsky

When the Puppet show is done right, the audience never sees the Puppet Master. Only when the show is over, and the illusion is complete, does he come forth at the sound of applause to meet. One must be aware of the Strings, which lead out of Sight, for it is in the awareness of the strings, where the Mind is guided Right. You are born a magician, you are born with the tools to create heaven on earth, don't let others create their heaven by keeping you in hell. You're your life energy to walk the path of self-mastery. Unless you have achieved self-realization, don't become anyone else's leader because they will fall over the cliff. Until we can lead, we must first begin to see reality for what it is. To be someone else's leader means to show them the light, by pointing it in the right direction; it is them who must walk it.

## S39 STRAWMAN – LEGAL ILLUSION BINDING YOU TO THIS PRISON

### *What/Who is the STRAWMAN?*

Every being who travels with their legal documents, carries anywhere they go said documents, or believes to be the NAME and the LAST NAME on the legal documents, is a slave by default. The legal documentation is created the moment the baby is born. The baby, before the umbilical cord is cut, is still attached to the mother. The baby is between two worlds, the physical and metaphysical one (inside the womb, is considered metaphysical because the baby has not been touched/polluted yet by the outside of the womb world). The moment the waters of the mother are out, the baby is considered merchandise for the legal system, but not until you apply for their birth certificate. Why would you need a birth certificate? The baby is already born, what more proof is there needed for the baby's existence? The reason for the legal documents is slavery, simple as that.

From the birth certificate, many other legal documentation is created throughout the person's life such as, school, marriage, death, mortgages, fines, insurances etc. All these are legal, but they don't apply to the baby (or the adult), they apply to the STRAWMAN, the name and last name on the legal documents. By believing that you are that person on the documents, you pay taxes and anything else that the government charges.

Everyone's legal documents (the name and the last name) are Crown copyrighted. By using legal documents, you are committing fraud. But they don't tell you this, they allow you to commit the fraud every time you use your STRAWMAN's information, because it benefits them. They are the whales who horde wealth and power on your behalf without giving you anything. Have you noticed that your legal documents have an expiry date? The plastic/paper cards and anything on them expire until they are renewed. But you, the living person never expire (except your physical body after the very last breath), so why pretend to be who you are not? You are not a strawman, you are the zygote. The zygote moment is the true moment of your birth/existence.

I have news for you, the government doesn't have money. They never did. All of their operations are done by using your money. Your birth certificate should have a unique registration number, which then it is used in the worldwide stock exchange. Since birth, your birth certificate has made millions or billions (depending on your age) of dollars. There is no reason as to why poverty should exist in the world. Paying taxes is a scam or anything else from the government (pertaining to the STRAWMAN) is a deception/scam. I used the word "government", but the puppet masters, the real government lurks in the shadows.

A fetus and its membranes is a delivery, when they don't deliver the umbilical cord and the placenta, that's not a delivery but an abortion. So, almost everyone is born incomplete/aborted. That abortion, the undelivered placenta is what creates the legal documentation. This is a long subject which if you are interested to know more about, which you should, read this book:

***You Are Not a Strawman You Are The Zygote***
by **Saimir X. Kercanaj**

## S40 WHAT YOU SAY, YOU BECOME

Pay attention to how you express (and think consciously) yourself mentally and verbally. The subconscious mind is our true state. Yes, we operate consciously, but we are simply replaying what's recorded in the subconscious mind. It is very important to record positive affirmation in the subconscious mind by expressing ourselves daily, by making positive statements where there is no room for doubt to anything we think, say or do.

| OK | BEST | WORST |
|---|---|---|
| Nothing is going to happen to me | I am safe, I'm secure. I am invincible. | I'm afraid. I'm worried. |
| I don't lack anything | My life is abundant | I don't have enough |
| I cannot get sick | I'm healthy at all times | I'm sick |
| I won't die any time soon | I'm immortal. I am created to be eternal | I am afraid of dying. I'm scared of death. |

The words on the right column "**WORST**" must not exist in your vocabulary. You can't have it both ways. You can't push and pull at the same time. Mind your language, live a self-aware life. Anything you say can become your life or your deathbed/tomb. With the words in the column "**BEST**", you are making a positive statement.

# S41 ESCAPE THE REINCARNATON CYCLE THROUGH THE HOLE IN THE GRID

**HOW TO ESCAPE THE CYCLE OF RE–INCARNATION ONCE AND FOR ALL**

If the after life is immortality, then having a purpose here could be an illusion; a deception which keeps us reincarnating, since most humans never accomplish in one lifetime what they need to, therefore, when they pass away, in the astral, when they are met with the beings (Archons disguised as relatives, parents etc.), people feel guilty for not having finished their work on the Earthly plane, therefore they reincarnate again here. Do not fall for it. Nobody can force you to come back here against your will. Unless you are doubtful and are still attached to people or pets or any other addictions on Earthly dimension/plane, will you then fall into the Archonic/Archontic deception, whether you meet the Archons directly or whether you are magnetized toward the Earthly plane and its unnatural toxic addictions.

---

The Great independent researcher, Wes Penre, in his book, **"Battles Between Shadow and Light"** teaches these 3 simple things to do/say on how to escape this reality/prison. Read these three points as if you are going to do and say (*which you are going to do and say them anyway, if you wish to escape the murder room a.k.a Earthly realm*) what needs to be said and done. Practice the three points daily so that you become entangled with it.

**1-** When I die, I will look "up" in relation to my deceased human body, and I will spot the Grid above me (a fuzzy net surrounding the Earth, having holes in it).

**2-** I spot one of the many holes in the Grid and I think along these lines, *"I am going through a hole in the Grid NOW!"* The astral is immediately thought-responsive, so my thoughts will execute instantly. Therefore, the word **NOW!** is very important, or you create your own delay.

**3-** Once out of the Grid, I will immediately think, *"I am at the Orion Queen's Highest possible aspect NOW!"* I will be there in an instant, regardless of where she roams at that moment.

---

These three things to do/say to leave this Archonic captured realm, is the most important thing anyone could ever learn/do in their lives. Nobody wants to suffer; this Earth is not our home. It can't be. Nature is beautiful for what it is, but this life here is dim compared to our true home. Some souls can leave this prison by intention alone, without having to recite the above. But, you don't know when you will physically die, you don't consciously know how much progress your soul will make until the last breath, so it is better to recite the "exiting through the Grid verbal/mental talk" daily if you can, so that you become entangled to that thought pattern frequency.

Some people who are attached to money all life, when they pass away, their psyche/soul is entangled energetically to money, which is also energy, therefore, those souls will be tricked by the Archons, Reptilians/Draco to return here or even if they are not met by the previous aforementioned entities, the confused souls will willingly return again here because money is what is familiar to them. That's why detachment to Earthly things is very important, so that you can go elsewhere based on your soul's highest path. Most people think that Earth is the only thing that exists on a physical level.

Even if there wasn't any other spiritual dimension, wouldn't you want to reincarnate beyond Antarctica, or in the Arctic center (which is warm and not freezing cold as they have led most people to believe), or in the inner Earth? Let me put it this way, in this world there are rich and poor countries. I mean the people, but as far as resources, every country is rich. Millions of people were born in poverty/poor countries, while many others in developed countries. Now, see the known official earth as one poor country where people reincarnate over and over again here. What if beyond Antarctica and the other places I mentioned earlier, there are continents where people are happy, free, and don't need to work? Why do the controllers of this realm hold Antarctica's borders so tight, not allowing the regular people to go beyond? The same applies for the Arctic center or the so-called North Pole.

No matter what you've done here, you are not obligated to return here, but you must have made peace with all you've done, all your wrongdoings (killing, backstabbing, lies, deception, greed, having abused your body or others, addicted to food, drinks, materialistic objects and other riches etc.). Don't think that you will end your life so that you can escape this Archontic Matrix. If you suicide, your whole being will be in chaos and confused. To escape this Matrix through the grid, one must have a clear mind, be determined and take NO for an answer. Archons and their minions are more powerful than you, ONLY if you believe so. To me, they are parasites, leeches.

Recite daily the simple passages (1, 2 and 3) about escaping the Matrix from the Grid. Just like you were bombarded with lies for a long time, likewise you must bombard yourself with truth. Everyday we can be distracted from all angels, and it's easy to forget the mission, which is to 'leave the body', meaning to escape this dense physical realm.

Archons can shapeshift to anything, such as Jesus, Mohamed, Buddha, your relatives, children, parents, or anyone you intimately loved while on Earth. Detachment to Earthly things is crucial to escaping this prison realm once and for all.

Having any attachment is like being tied to a rope like a dog and trying to go farther than the end of the rope. It is impossible.

## S42 DO NOT GO TOWARD THE LIGHT (MOON), IT IS A TRAP

When you pass away, DO NOT go toward the Moon/The Light tunnel, that is the Moon being used as a trap to get you to return/reincarnate again here, with amnesia (with completely wiped out memories). When you pass away, you will feel like you are in complete darkness (because you are not living/finding yourself in anymore to what is familiar to you). Imagine finding yourself in the woods at night, by yourself. If somewhere in the distance there is a light shining, logic and the will to survive would tell you to go toward the light. Again, do not go toward the light. It is very important for you to understand that the spirit is eternal, there is no death. When you understand this, then you shouldn't have any problem ignoring the Light/tunnel, or anyone else pretending to be someone who cares about you.

Is it possible that the Moon's pull is one of the causes that caused women to menstruate (on top of unhygienic living and through ordinary intercourse, as opposed to procreating through 'parthenogenesis')? This logic  (about menstruation) is based on the times before there was a Moon here, when civilizations thrived spiritually, with no wars, no suffering and no diseases. Loving people, animals etc. is good, but don't be attached to anyone or anything. That is the solution/requirement (beside eliminating fear) to have a big chance in escaping this Archontic prison.

Some may ask the question:

**QUESTION** - "Since it's easy to escape through the Grid by simply saying 'I am going through a hole in the Grid NOW, then I won't bother to work on myself (becoming self-disciplined), exercise, helping others, etc. Why work hard on myself when I can simply recite this sentence?"

**ANSWER** - Wrong! For you to be able to escape this Matrix, you have to have a clear mind, an open heart, fearlessness, no worries etc. Your Spirit must be tempered with bravery and sovereignty. Otherwise, you will be too weak, fragmented and you will easily be tricked by the Archons. Unless, the Archons are too busy watching astral TV (joking), to pay attention to you trying to escape their claws. Sleep exists only here in this realm. The physical body sleeps, the spirit or the astral body never does.

In the above (ANSWER), I mentioned "opened heart". You may say that how can the heart exist in the astral realm? As above So below can also relate to both physical and non physical reality. For any organs that you have here, there is an equal organ in the astral realm. Do not mistake the astral realm as invisible. It is visible when you are there, it's just not as dense as this realm here. You can take any form you wish. If you want to become a ship and fly in the air, you can do that. Do you want to become a Light Orb and travel that way? You can do that too, and anything else you wish. Only here in this realm the weight of our body keeps us down. Earth is beautiful in her (Mother Earth is feminine) own right, but there are much more beautiful places out there, without having to work, suffer and anything else we have down here. I say "down here" in relation to the sky, the luminaries and stars which are portals. There are civilizations out there, not only by going up and through the portals (Sun, and the other so called planets a.k.a. .luminaries), but also within the Earth, below us. We are below in relation to the sky, but we are also above, in relation to the inner Earth's 6D (6$^{th}$ dimension).

If you astral travel or if you lucid dream, you cannot go beyond 5D reality. To go beyond that, one must **leave** the body or **disconnect**, both terms describe the same thing. You are always connected to the divine. You will just disconnect from this prison.

## S43 CAN A DISEASED PERSON CROSS OVER OR ESCAPE THE MATRIX?

If you are in a wheelchair, or if you are vaccinated or any other thing you might think will prohibit you from crossing over, it is false. You can still escape this prison or harsh school, but have in mind that when you are met with the shapeshifting Archons, there must be no doubts in your mind, you must be fearless and say "NO" if they try to trick you (or attempt you in any way) into getting back in this reality again. The moment you pass away, you are perfectly healthy. No more diseases. If you are blind, deaf, on a wheelchair etc. while on Earth, if you pass away, those hindrances are gone.

The ability to cross over is within everyone. The potential and right to everything one desires is there, it is everyone's right. There are beings (evil factions of Archons, Reptilians, Greys etc.) out there who are devoid of empathy, they live in a materialistic mindset, their heart is enslaved by the mind. Their deceptions and tactics have poisoned many of us as we can see it in our society where there are fights, anger and hate between family members, friends, in work places etc. Emotional chaos keeps someone enslaved to this reality, and it will be very difficult for some to cross over when the time comes.

> Jacques Attali, in 1981, wrote: "The future will be about finding a way to reduce the population. We start with the old, because as soon as they exceed 60-65 years of age, people live longer than they produce and that costs society dearly. Then the weak, then the useless that do not help society because there will always be more of them, and above all, ultimately, the stupid. Euthanasia targeting these groups; Euthanasia will have to be an essential tool in our future societies, in all cases. Of course we will not be able to execute people or build camps. We get rid of them by making them believe that it is for their own good. Overpopulation, and mostly useless, is something that it is too costly economically. Socially, too, it is much better when the human machine comes to an abrupt standstill than when it gradually deteriorates. Neither will we be able to test millions upon millions of people for their intelligence. We will find or cause something, a pandemic, targeting certain people, a real economic crisis or not, a virus affecting the old or the fat, it doesn't matter, the weak will succumb to it, the fearful and stupid will believe in it and seek treatment. We will have made sure that treatment is in place, treatment that will be the solution. The selection of idiots then takes care of itself; You go to the slaughter by yourself". *Jacques Attali has written a few books but they are in French* .

Education a.k.a. the indoctrination system/schools and people willing to be injected with toxic poison thinking it will heal them, proves that they were able to test populations' intelligence. Personally, I don't believe in viruses, but in a severely weakened immune system/protection mechanism. There are good and bad bacteria. The bad bacteria always looks for its comfortable and natural habitat, which is a polluted body with parasites, bacteria etc. A body which is clean and healthy will repel any bad bacteria or toxicity.

## S44 VACCINES INJURIES ARE NORMALIZED DECEPTIVELY - UNFORTUNATELY

Vaccine injuries are not rare, people have been programmed to think that neurological disorders, autoimmune disorders, allergies, ear infections, seizures, eczema and fevers are normal. 'Normal' is dangerous. Because something is seen as normal by most people, does not mean that it is the truth. One very simple example as to how easy it is to program a person to deny nature is by telling them that nuts are dangerous (speaking of those who are allergic to them). You cannot be allergic to natural food in its most natural form such as nuts, fruits, vegetables etc.

The allergy happens because the internal environment is polluted with chemicals from the vaccines, air (chemtrails), cell phone towers (including technological devices you use inside your home) etc. Even if you are not allergic to anything, it doesn't mean that it won't get you. Any damage done to the body is accumulative. The cells in the body work at their highest capacity all the time until they give up. When they give up, the health of the person deteriorates very fast.

Whatever you do, do not vaccinate your children, definitely not the infants. Many parents, when the child has an ear pain or an infection, they rush to the hospital. It's understandable, no parent wants their children to get sick or die. But going to the mainstream hospital or doctors, it's as if the cow would willingly go to be slaughtered. Mainstream doctors are not taught to treat patients with natural cures such as herbs, essential oils, music therapy, singing and many other natural effective ways. They are taught to treat their patients with antibiotics and other toxic chemicals. In this day and age, with so much great information available to us all, it is sad and irresponsible to treat ourselves with chemicals.

## S45 CAN THE VACCINATED SOULS BE ELIMINATED OR WILL THEY BE FOREVER TRAPPED IN THE REINCARNATION CYCLE/TRAP?

*"In the future, we (he is speaking of THEM, the monsters who aim for the negative timeline New World Order) will eliminate the soul with medicine. Under the pretext of a "healthy point of view", there will be vaccines by which the human body will be treated as soon as possible directly at birth, so that the human being cannot develop the thought of the existence of Soul and Spirit.*

*The materialistic doctors will be entrusted with the task of removing the soul of humanity. As today, people are vaccinated against this disease or that disease, so in the future, children will be vaccinated with a substance that can be produced precisely in such a way that people, thanks to this vaccination, will be immune to being subjected to the "madness" of spiritual life. He would be extremely smart, but he would not develop a conscience, and that is the true goal of some materialistic circles.*

*With such a vaccine, you can easily make the etheric body loose in the physical body. Once the etheric body is detached, the relationship between the universe and the etheric body would become extremely unstable, and man would become an automaton, for the physical body of man must be polished on this Earth by spiritual will.*

*So, the vaccine becomes a kind of **aryman**ique force; man can no longer get rid of a given materialistic feeling. He becomes materialistic of the constitution and can no longer rise to the spiritual".* – Rudolph Steiner (1861-1925)

The above was written over 100 years ago. And you think they haven't managed to separate/suppress many people's etheric bodies/ souls? Look at society, for many people, materialism is God. Their souls have been captured.

In parenthesis, in the above quote, I called the controllers "monsters". The truth is that there are monsters also among us. How many people hurt and brutalize each other? If controllers or monsters exist, that's because monsters exist within ourselves. I know countless people (many of them are siblings or so-called friends) who backstab each other, argue and fight over money, land and other man-made nonsense. To get rid of the monsters outside of ourselves, we must first tame the monster within.

In his reference to an "arymanique force" Steiner is referring to Ahriman, a diabolical entity from ancient Persian mythology who was seen as Lord of the material world. Steiner warned that Ahriman would incarnate in human form in the latter part of the twentieth century; when he would be very active in the realm of modern banking and science.

Today Christians would see Ahriman as Satan. Ahriman is the personification of "destructive spirit" in Zoroastrianism. Ahriman is the evil spirit in Early Iranian Religion, Zoroastrianism and Zorvanism. He is the Lord of Darkness Chaos and the source of human confusion. Just as Asmodeus is the evil spirit or the Prince of Lust which controls many men and women through pornography and sexualization.

Ahriman would be the antithesis of Christ. Steiner warned, insofar as he (Ahriman) wanted to lock man entirely in the physical realm. In contrast to Christ who sought to liberate mankind spiritually.

## S46 Who is AHRIMAN?

"He is the demon of demons, and dwells in an abyss of endless darkness in the north, the traditional home of the demons. Ignorance, harmfulness, and disorder are the characteristics of Ahriman. He can change his outward form and appear as a lizard, a snake, or a youth. His aim is always to destroy the creation of [Ahura Mazda] and to this end he follows behind the creator's work, seeking to spoil it. As Ahura Mazda creates life, Ahriman creates death; for health, he produces disease; for beauty, ugliness. All man's ills are due entirely to Ahriman" - *Scholar*, John R. Hinnels

That's why Ahriman would be especially active in the fields of banking and scientific materialism, two areas of human activity where his influence is particularly strong. Through his influence in these fields Ahriman would be able to deny humanity its spiritual birthright on the pretext of "health" and "science".

Rudolf Steiner was an Austrian occultist, social reformer, architect, esotericist, and clairvoyant. Steiner gained initial recognition at the end of the nineteenth century as a literary critic and published works including The Philosophy of Freedom. At the beginning of the twentieth century he founded an esoteric spiritual movement, anthroposophy, with roots in German idealist philosophy and theosophy.

The Waldorf Schools are based on Rudolf Steiner's work. The main reason for the vaccination is to remove the soul from the body. Or to keep it chained/suppressed forever. Know that what you think is impossible, it is indeed possible. But the difference between death and life is in your ability to act based on your soul's inner divine calling. The only power that the dark magicians may have over you is if you think/believe that they are more powerful. They are as powerful or as weak as you allow them to be.

There is nobody that puts in charge anyone over you. It's only our ignorance who caused us to find ourselves in this situation. He who doesn't know himself, is doomed to suffer. Throughout this book I use the term 'dark magicians'. I refer to the evil spirit/s, to the ones who coerce and threaten humanity by using nefarious and deceptive tactics to exercise control over humanity.

You may have a question in your mind such as, "If after we pass away we are perfectly healthy, why would the controllers (Archons/ Shadow governments) want to poison us with toxic foods, drinks, immoral content etc.? They know they can't keep us here forever, since when we die (in this realm) we are not sick anymore. Here's the answer. By poisoning you with foods and drinks, by filling up your mind with toxic thoughts (which eventually lead to detrimental physical actions) through porn, movies, TV shows, Magazines, so-called traditions, religions etc., your psyche/soul will be exhausted, and confused, so that when the person passes away, they are easily sent back through the reincarnation cycle. Make amends with anything and anyone that will keep you trapped and tied into this prison. Even if you don't wish to meet someone that hurt you, for the purpose of making amends, you can forgive them in your heart. Is just as valid as if you told them in person. Even if that person doesn't know it consciously, their soul does. Thoughts and feelings are astral substances, thoughts and feelings know neither space nor time; they are instantaneous.

Do you remember when you previously read this "*I am going through a hole in the Grid NOW!*" ? The word 'NOW!' is the most important thing to say that can instantly take you where you need to be. If you don't, then any second that you delay, you are prone to trickery. And even if you are not met with any Archons (as themselves or shapeshifted as your relatives, Jesus, Buddha, Krishna, pets, siblings etc.), you may be surrounded with fear and confusion, for the fact that you will be surrounded by uncertainties, since the only certain/ familiar thing you will remember is, life here on Earth.

Your thoughts have power. Instantly you can ignore them (*assuming anyone tries to meet you, greet you or any other way of contacting you*) and leave through one of the openings of the Grid or the Forcefield. They can do nothing to you, they cannot stop you when you are fearless. Do not let them use your life's mistakes against you. It is of paramount importance that you forgive yourself (by beginning now) of all the mistakes you've done in life and learnt from them. So that you don't feel any guilt when Archons use your life's mistakes to trap you into feeling guilty.

There is a chance you may not meet any Archons or anyone else trying to deceive you. But that chance depends on how much progress you've made while alive, that's why it is important to begin forgiving anyone you've done wrong to and anyone that did wrong to you. Forgiving someone that you are still in a relationship with means that they have changed, otherwise you must leave them. Your life is your responsibility. Don't let anyone hold you down/back.

If you are attached to alcohol, porn/sex, pets, humans, politics, religions, sport, nationality, money, materialistic riches, ideologies or anything Earthly, you'll come back here; you will reincarnate again without memories. Don't let emotions confuse your rational mind. Listen to the inner voice, do you want to repeat this life again?

Orgasms, not only that they shorten your life, but they will also act as portals for Archontic low frequency thought fields/patterns to possess you. Archons are cunning. They possess you incrementally where you think it's you that thinks your thoughts. Do you think your thoughts are actually yours? They can be yours, but which way do you lean, what are your daily choices, what do you eat, what do you drink? Parasites (physical or non physical entities) can enter in you through the skin, mouth (especially alcohol, no matter the amount), genital organs, eyes, ears and astrally (through orgasm/climaxes).

## S47 IN THE ASTRAL REALM, YOU CAN GO ANYWHERE INSTANTLY

Before you're about to fall asleep, your brain is in Alpha brain wave, you are in that drowsy state where you can visualize anything, and can travel anywhere instantly. This happens to me every time before falling asleep. That same state (but on a more powerful level) can happen when you are meditating deeply or when you pass away. When you pass away after having made peace with anyone and anything that you have harmed or been harmed from, therefore, you are not confused. If you are not confused, the Archons cannot trick you into the reincarnation cycle. If you are not confused, you can easily go through the field/barrier or the electromagnetic Grid.

Depending on your soul's progress, one may even choose to leave their body while asleep. Meaning that the body/person will die in this realm, but the soul has chosen or found out how to escape the Matrix while asleep. Note that only the physical body sleeps, the soul is always awake.

**IMPORTANT**: Suicide is not an answer. If it was, then everyone would have suicided and escaped this Archon controlled realm. Suiciding brings you automatically back here. Taking your own life has to do with the Divine Law. Nobody can infringe on natural law. Do not get confused with man-made law, they are two different laws, one is real/true that operates at all times how it should, while the other can be manipulated and altered as humans see fit.

## S48 CYBORG HUMANITY

Their agenda is to create a biological immortal cyborg humanity. But humanity without free will. That's what the vaccination (which includes nanotechnology) is for. It replaces the fire in the blood (soul) with this new synthetic robotic substance. If you are vaccinated, do not panic, your divine will is more powerful than any man-made or Archonic made synthetic technology. Your divine will and intention, when spoken, thought and acted from a higher frequency, can eliminate anything of lower frequency.

One must practice his or her divine will with full conviction. But "thought" alone is not enough, one must also pay attention to what they eat or drink. What you eat or drink dictates the purity of your blood/soul. Even if you eat and drink perfectly healthy, there is still something else, equally important, which most people neglect or don't know. And that is, "sexual continence". Continence means to contain your sexual energy, to not waste it. Anytime you ejaculate, menstruate, have ordinary sex, masturbate or climax/orgasm, your soul's fire diminishes.

With a weakened soul, when you pass away, you won't be too strong to escape the pull of the Moon's and Archon's deceptive tactics. You are free to believe this or not. I know what I know and that is good enough for me. And because I fully understand the importance of sharing ultimate knowledge (which is the Greatest gift), I'm sharing it with you. I am not separate from you. I am YOU. You are ME. Do you get it? We are each other playing this game on Earth called life. Unfortunately, THEY hijacked Earth, and changed the rules of the game, rules that only they benefit from.

The sooner you understand this subject (escaping the Matrix) and practice it, the sooner our race will be free. The Cyborg race may come to pass or may not. Even if it does, it will be its own reality/timeline. If you are reading this, you WILL NOT have the displeasure to live in that fully tyrannical society. You will either live in another beautiful realm, according to your spirit's soul life path, or you may decide to reincarnate in another realm entirely. That is up to you to know, but to know, you must first get out of the state of amnesia. And to get out of that state, you must leave this realm.

When you leave your body, if you wish, you can incarnate in a "Garden of Eden" like reality. In our world, some are born in very poor families where they struggle all their life and some are born in families where their life is easy. Prepare yourself so that you choose which portal you'll go through, the FALSE WHITE LIGHT (Moon) which will bring you back here or in a different reality where civilizations thrive spiritually.

Never forget that you are a spirit, but you have a body. You are not your body. As above so below, the Grid (Earthly prison) is "As Above", and your physical body is, "So Below". Just as your physical body, "As Above", your cells inside of you are, "So Below". Everything is repeated in cycles, sizes and realities **MACRO**cosmically and **MICRO**cosmically.

## S49 FEAR OF THE UNKNOWN BRINGS YOU BACK

Don't be scared of the unknown (life beyond this reality here). It is called "unknown" because you forgot about it and you see it as "unknown". If your mother was in prison and gave birth to you, and if you were raised in a prison, the prison would be the only thing you knew and you couldn't think or believe that there is life beyond the prison. But if you face your fears and doubts, you will find out that there is life beyond the prison walls (literally-physical prison cell, and metaphorically, beyond the mental prison bars). Just as when you were in your mothers belly, where it was the only home you knew, not knowing what was outside of it (speaking metaphorically here, as the spirit knows what is outside of the **WOMB**an).

Another scenario for the souls of this creation is that those who fail to ascend (most people will ascend), will become immortal, but with no free will. Their souls will be enslaved forever. The laser-like spiritual/synthetic man-made a.k.a Archonic technology can penetrate one's soul with ease. Not just anyone but those people who refused to awaken and raise their frequency to the point that escaping this Matrix once and for all becomes a reality. That time will be from 2030-2060.

It will be a transitioning period, just as we have been in the transitioning period for a while, but in 2011 it began to ramp up. Currently we are walking two parallel timelines, one which frees us and one which enslaves us forever, meaning the NEW WORLD ORDER (the negative timeline). But there is also a positive timeline NEW WORLD ORDER. If you ask most people what they think the New World Order means, they will answer that it is the negative timeline, that's because people's minds have been conditioned to think and believe so. We create the timeline that we want. There is nothing to be afraid of, you just work on yourself, raise your frequency, act through self awareness, think and speak from a higher consciousness state of mind. Help one another, love one another, appreciate and be grateful for your body (mind and spirit), for the world, animals, people and creation in general.

The dates I wrote earlier are not set in stone. But things point out at that time frame, if not earlier. Time to convince others and try to awaken them is done. Do not waste anymore time, you can only warn them, if they ignore you or refuse to listen to you, move on, your life if your responsibility as is everyone's life and happiness their own responsibility.

## S50 SHAPESHIFTING BLUEBLOODS

Why do you think that meat, especially pig/pork is a popular food (actually death), especially in North America? They have been preparing humanity to accept cannibalism (even if it's eaten cooked), not just for humans to become sick, full of parasites, but for the shapeshifters also, to consume human flesh. If a shapeshifter, reptilian/blueblood species consumed a human that is of a higher vibration, it wouldn't work. A high frequency being is full of light, meanwhile a monster race is full of death/parasites. It will conflict, just like people of all blood types cannot give blood to everyone, no matter the blood type.

Pork is a genetic hybrid creation of a wild boar and human. Genetic modification between different species of humans and animals, or any other combinations have existed at least since we were first created. By "WE", I mean any and all species that have existed in this realm which is Archon controlled.

**If you know anyone who eats meat and enjoys it, their blood is slowly being replaced into a copper like, just like Archons' or Reptilians' blood.** I'm not trying to spread fear mongering; I'm trying to bring awareness. Shapeshifting species have existed for a long time. I wasn't even going to write anything on Archons or Reptilians, but at the same time I felt obligated to let you know that they are the ones who feed on our suffering, sickness and disease and fear and terror. Sometimes I hear people saying that how can they feed themselves from fear without food?

First of all, they don't necessarily need to consume solid food. Depending on which faction we're talking about (there are different layers of shapeshifters just as there are humans that need to eat a lot, others who barely eat, and those who are breatharians), the higher, more intelligent faction/group can sense the fear and terror that humans go through. Their technology supplies them, by syphoning populations' fear and emotional chaos.

> "*A clear thought, a powerful word*
> *and a self-aware action of love and*
> *care a day, starves the shapeshifters*
> *and keeps them away*" – Arolv Jae

## S51 ONES AND ZEROES – WOMBan & MAN, ARE WE ANDROGYNOUS?

In this physical Matrix, anything created, has first been initiated in our Divine Minds, equivalent to Spirit, which is feminine. In the occult (occult means hidden, many people mistakenly assume that occult means cult) teachings '0' symbolizes the female genital and '1' symbolizes the male genital. An idea manifests outwardly. Out of 0 comes 1. The 1 denotes the physical manifestation. Man (physical man and woman) comes from the WOMBan/as below (the 0, the Spirit world). But also the man and the woman come from the Spirit world which is a WOMB/female. The computer code functions in 1s and 0s, which is based on the creation of the female genital '0' and the erected male genital '1'.

The nose is sticking out (male), but it has holes (feminine), the same applies to the ears. The penis sticks out, but it has a hole (feminine). The vagina is a hole but it has the clitoris (male). This is on a microcosmic level which applies here in the Matrix. Anywhere else including this reality, every being is androgynous. As an example, **if you are a man, why do you think you have nipples? If you are a woman, why do you think you have a clitoris**?

Occult symbolism is everywhere in the world, one example is the obelisk. How is an obelisk shaped? Like a male penis of course. There are obelisks in Rome, U.S.A. and many other places in the world as monuments in big or smaller cities. They symbolize patriarchy, meaning that the controller's favourite system is patriarchy, because through that system they control people's mind. By suppressing women, and female energy in men, people will then live in the **m**ind (physical Matrix; attached to materialism) and not in the **M**ind (Spirit world; connected with our innermost Divine Selves). You won't find any Ankh monuments in the world. You may find depictions or engravings in walls but not erected monuments by the patriarchal controllers. The ankh symbol represents both Man and Woman in unity, The Ankh has both the 1 and the 0

The image on the left is the Ankh symbol representing the masculine and feminine energy in balance, while the other three images (obelisks) represent only the masculine energy, a.k.a. patriarchy. The Ankh has both the 1 and the 0. While the obelisk is simply just '1'. The female and male are presented in so many different levels. The one eye or *The All Seeing Eye of Providence*, if flipped on the side, symbolizes the female genital leading into the birth canal. The female genital is the source of life, the WOMBan creates life out of nowhere (from our physical perspective) but actually from SOMEWHERE else, the source of all, the Great Spirit).

What does the top of the eye (when flipped ) look like? It looks like the clitoris. Coincidence? I think not. There are no coincidences or mistakes in the Divine Creation, there are only synchronicities. The iris looks like a black hole on a microcosmic level, just as on a macrocosmic level there is the Black Hole, the Source of All, the Zero Point where everything begins and ends (actually recycles, restarts, expansion etc.).

## S52 ARE "A.I. CONSCIOUS" HUMANS ALREADY AMONG US?

Have you noticed that in our world there are a lot of people that no matter how much truth or common sense you present to them, they are still oblivious? What could that be? Are they unactivated (not activated yet) A.I. cyborgs? Could the plan be that their children will be fully activated and take over the world where there would not be anymore people thinking for themselves? Again, this is not fear mongering. It is better to be prepared. A few people I know (and myself in the past) try so hard to awaken some family members that it seems like they do not want to wake up. To be a good hearted "Man Being" (human) is a must, but it shouldn't override the rational mind. By knowing that those beings who refuse to awaken, could be A.I. powered biological cyborgs, then you know to not waste anymore time with them, it is better to move on and help others in need for knowledge or any other help.

They prepare humanity to accept these A.I. conscious robots, which are indistinguishable from you or me, at least on a physical level. They prepare humanity by normalizing the idea through movies, Tv shows, magazines, ads and videogames. Speaking of video games, there's this video game which I played years ago (when I used to play videogames) called, 'Detroit Become Human'. You play as the A.I. powered robot which looked exactly like us, they just had some glowing technological circle on the left side of the head, the only thing that made them look different from a regular human. The story is made in such a way to make you sympathize and feel sorry for the robots/humans like cyborgs. I beat the game of course, it had a great story (choice driven story, one wrong choice and your character would be dead for the rest of the game), but I was constantly analyzing it and I knew why they were doing it.

They either create conscious biological cyborgs in the lab, or they turn a regular human into an unconscious A.I. person, provided they injected (through various ways) people with nanotechnology. If you are vaccinated, refuse to believe that you will turn into a robot without free will. When your intention is of a higher frequency, nothing can harm you. This does not mean that you have to throw yourself in harm's way. Avoid anything and anyone that lowers your frequency. A lot of people are not vaccinated and yet, they behave as if they were. INTENTION is everything.

# S53 THREE MAJOR SHOCKERS THAT WILL TRIGGER THE GROWTH OF NEW BRAIN CELLS

**1)** <u>Fasting</u> - Fasting plays a major role in the creation of new neural pathways. When you fast for at least 18 hours, the body goes into shock and it will create new brain cells. Not just in the brain but everywhere in the body, but 18h is the minimum. At 72h of fasting, max autophagy is achieved. Make sure the last meal is no later than 4 or 5Pm (16:00 or 17:00), this way when you go to bed, your last meal contents will have been digested by then. If you eat late and if you go to bed before the food in your stomach is digested, then the body will use its energy for the digestion process as opposed to healing and renewing your brain cells or cells elsewhere in the body.

If you are anemic, you should not attempt long fasts until you are ready for it. And to be ready for it, raw/natural food consumption is a must. Through fruit and vegetable consumption you will receive all 12 mineral salts that the body requires to function properly.

**2)** <u>Cold shower</u>. Finish the warm/hot shower with a cold one. That is a great shocker. Your body will go into shock and will initiate the production of new brain cells. If you cannot do this immediately, train yourself gradually, from hot to not so cold, then next time from hot to a little bit more cold and finally from hot to full cold. But the ultimate test is to always have a cold shower no matter what season it is. But that is an advanced step. Just as when you want to dry fast you must first go through the lower levels first.

**3)** H.I.I.T – **H**igh **I**ntensity **I**nterval **T**raining is another major shocker. Exercise really hard for 30 seconds and then stop for a minute and then repeat. You could also run for your life for 30 seconds and then stop, take a break and repeat it a few times. We cannot grow in comfort. All these shockers fall in the discomfort category which are very good brain cell renewals but also beneficial to the whole body overall.

**STOP YOUR THOUGHTS ANYTIME YOU WISH**
Close your eyes (actually your eyelids), breathe deep and hold it. Look

up and then say mentally "What is my brain thinking now?". If you do it correctly, your thoughts will stop lurking in your mind. But do this when you are by yourself, and not tv or music on. It has to become a habit in practicing solitude. Most people create constantly in an unconscious state, not while sleeping, instead while awake but not really self-aware. We are ultimately spirited, but we have forgotten that because we are made amnesiac by external forces who drive and control the Matrix (the physical reality) system.

Creation happens instantly, which happens in our Divine Mind that belongs to the Great Spirit, compared to our conscious mind which belongs to the Matrix. If you want to get out of the Matrix as much as possible, daily, detach from physical reality by meditation, deep breathing, solitude etc. To not create havoc in our lives, we must also use our free will to withhold manifesting what we don't want to manifest in the moment. There is a right time and place for everything. Just because we can create with our Divine Mind, it doesn't mean that we shouldn't care who we destroy in the process.

# PART THREE
## THE TRUE DIVINE SELF

# S O U L

"All men's souls are immortal, but the souls of the righteous, are immortal and divine" – **Socrates**

Happiness is a quality of the soul; not a function of one's material circumstances" – **Aristotle**

"If only our eyes saw souls instead of bodies, how very different our ideas of beauty would be"

> **"The soul, like the body, accepts by practice
> whatever habit one wishes it to contact"**
> *- Socrates*

D on't give your DNA to corporations to discover your ancestral background. Because now you can be framed for any crime. If they can, they will. In some jobs, the workers are given an alleged drug test with a swab thing you keep in the mouth for what seemed like 1/2 hour. If you are one of them you'll regret doing this. They will clone you or use it to make limited (limited on purpose) self-aware robots. A real drug test would just collect urine or hair samples. Don't give up hair clippings anymore either for reasons like being framed or cloned. Urine, hair, blood or any part of your body has your DNA, which in the wrong hands it can be used for nefarious reasons. There are more malevolent reasons for your DNA to be used rather than good reasons. A good reason is that they can create a new liver or kidney or heart for you, if one of your organs was beyond repair. But this would apply only if the healthcare system was genuine and for the people but that's not the case.

Technically, they got your DNA at birth, depending on which country you were born in. In some countries they are more heartless than others. But since your birth, times have changed for the worse, mainstream institutions have become more corrupt than before. This means that the system collapses when the governments become more tyrannical. Regardless if they have your DNA or not, we must practice sovereignty, being self aware and disobeying tyranny. It's one thing to obey from not knowing and another if you know. Now you know that authorities don't have your best interest. Money, riches and power corrupts one's soul. Authoritarian figures are all corrupted with the exception of those who have infiltrated the tyrannical system to destroy it from within.

THEY (the dark evil powers) have paid very close attention to OUR blood (anytime you go for a blood test). This is how THEY categorize us all! How do you think our SS numbers work? THEY are waiting for just one to figure out who (*anyone with Christ lineage or even \*Christ himself, assuming he would reincarnate again on a different body as a regular person but with the same blood/consciousness*) he is and how he reacts. Through blood tests they find those with super powers, even though some people are oblivious to their dormant super powers, and then through different means they take that person and who knows what they do to them. Many people are kidnapped for all sorts of reasons.

*Personally, I believe that we all are Chrystic beings. But what I meant here is that they look for those with very powerful untainted DNA. If you drink alcohol  eat meat, watch porn, lie, deceive, hold onto grudge, gossip, envy, afraid, worries etc., they don't care about you because you are already in their trap, but if you are an open-hearted person, think for yourself, are appreciative/grateful person etc., you are danger to them because they don't want you to awaken other people. The more awakened people are, the more difficult for THEM to control humans. I'm using the word "humans" but we are actually Astral Beings. We live here on Earth, but we are not of "Earth".

Many people get wrongfully convicted. Could it be that they swap DNA between people? Do you think the justice system wouldn't wrongly convict people? It is laughable for it to be called "The Justice System". It is anything but "justice".

_____

Read the book "*YOU ARE NOT A STRAWMAN; YOU ARE THE ZYGOTE*" by Saimir Kercanaj which I mentioned a few chapters earlier. Your legal name and last name is the STRAWMAN. Admitting to be the fictional entity a.k.a. the STRAWMAN puts you at a disadvantage. They can frame you however they want when you think and live as the legal name and last name. But if you don't admit to being the legal name and the last name, they cannot do anything to you. They trick you into admitting to be the NAME, that's the titan secret they had over the modern humans since 10 decades ago when the first birth certificate was issued for the first time. Read the book I just mentioned and you'll understand.

DNA is your EVERYTHING. It is your castle, don't let anyone interfere, intermingle with it, or in any way shape or form that would cause you to descend even further in consciousness.

In another book titled, *I Am The Key That Opens All Doors* by the same author, Saimir Kercanaj, wrote:

> "Your DNA is like a genie in a bottle except they are genes in your body. Connected to the unified field of the universe, they react to your thoughts to make your wishes a reality by attracting people, and experiences which you desire and think about most. Your DNA is your soul roadmap for where you have been energetic wise. Your DNA is a record of your past (in our linear way of inner standing TIME) incarnations during multiple phases of existence and parallel realities. From where you sit, the DNA is a testament to your evolutionary and karmic relationship with the universe"

## S55 REVERSE AGING - AGING IS A FALSE CONSTRUCT

You are created to last forever. Aging first began when we fell in consciousness. Before the fall, we didn't need anything external. Ether provided anything we needed. Because we lost connection with the divine, we had to rely on external sources for food and water. The more times passed, the more we were degenerating, to the point that our lifespan ended up being what it is now, on average 70-80 years of age. Before the fall we didn't need any man-made calendars or clocks. All we needed to know was in the sky, the movement of the celestial bodies told time.

Modern clocks and calendars have their useful uses of course, but people have become too reliant on them. Work environments contribute to aging. Besides the stress that most people experience working for corporations, just looking at the clock when you have to go to work, while on lunch, or before you go, contribute further to aging. Many people would ridicule this explanation but the internal cells of the human body listen to the main switch, which is 'you'.

Celebrating your or other people's birthdays is part of the aging process. We grow, we don't get old. Every time you use the word 'old' when talking about your age, you are further confirming to your trillions of cells to continue the self-destructing process . Everything begins in the mind. Anything you do or say in the physical reality, it first began in the mind. So does the aging begin and end, in the mind. Life happens in the moment; live in the moment and not in a supposed future which hasn't arrived yet.

Everything inflicted on us is our own doing. Perception doesn't mean 'truth'. What we perceive can be an illusion. Do away with the false beliefs/constructs and you will be able to discern false/illusion from truth. You become what you think, and what you think you become. The more you are engaging with something, the more entanglement will happen between you and "IT". It applies the same whether you engage in positivity or negativity. But of course, speaking of aging, you won't stop aging just by being positive about it.

The mind is one aspect, the other aspect is the body. If you feed your body with unnatural food and drinks, you will still age, even if you truly believe that you won't age. If you truly believe and feel that you don't age, if you consume perfectly healthy food, you will still age if you spill your life force a.k.a. semen, or ovum if you are a woman. Many men are familiar with saving their seeds since semen retention has gained momentum. But ovum retention is new, only a few women know, understand or practice it. Menopause clearly indicates that death will surely arrive. I already mentioned somewhere in this book about the 'Parthenogenesis' subject. Parthenogenesis means conception without sexual intercourse. That subject, plus how to cure menstruation and menopause are widely talked about in the book "Creation of the Superman" by Dr. Raymond W. Bernard (with commentary by Liquid Metal).

I love what Blake Cyrier wrote in his book "**NATURAL TREASURE – Quest for Knowledge, Health & Freedom**" about aging in the chapter *Principles Of Longevity p32*:

*"Old age, as we perceive it, is a construct of a mind clouded by false beliefs, a distorted dream far removed from our innate potential. Reject the notion that aging is an inevitable ticking of a clock. In the realm of eternity, time is but an illusion, a tool that may also be used to measure an accumulation of damage inflicted upon a mind and body.*

*The journey to becoming younger starts with rejecting our age, belief and faith in growing old. Next we must direct our efforts to diminish the toxic burden on both mind and body. The subsequent crusade is one of purification, a relentless endeavor to expel the toxic remnants of death that linger within, to clear the way for the essence of life".*

Two main reasons why people age, actually three reasons are: **Belief in aging, unhygienic diet and sexual incontinence**.

## 1- BELIEF IN AGING – WHAT YOU BELIEVE, WILL HAPPEN

*Birthdays* – Birthdays are dark rituals. On a surface level, birthdays seem like they are celebrations in a positive way. Unfortunately, they are not, they contribute to aging for the fact that thinking about your age number, cements certain death. Anything you think or believe strongly enough, will become your tomb, in this case celebrating your birthday. Grow like a tree as opposed to getting old. Many people think that aging is normal and that living to a 100 years of age is an achievement. That is absolute nonsense and sad at the same time. But, seeing it from the perspective of those people, they are right about their own life, but they think/believe that applies to everyone else.

A lot of presents (toxic toys or other materialistic junk), cakes and other toxic and harmful foods and drinks are consumed when there are birthday celebrations. For what, celebrating that someone got older? Think about it, how can you be happy to become older. Many people are enticed and feel like celebrating because, for a day or two or for a few hours, it would take them away from their struggling life. If our life is happy daily, why would we need to be happy at certain days of the year? Birthdays are distractions, poisons for the body and the mind. As if these were not enough, people ask "how OLD are you now?"; using the word 'old', cements the belief in getting old and aging.

*Waiting, thinking about retirement* – This is another culprit in contributing to aging faster and consequently failing physical death. Failed physical death means when you die with a corrupted soul where your next incarnation will be memory-less, because you will not remember the lessons and the experiences of your previous lifetime.

A lot of people think about their retirement because they are too tired of working, too tired of giving their life energy to this vampiric system. Opportunities to live without the need to work for a corporation are endless, especially on the internet. What's the point of life, have you ever asked yourself this question? Are you here just to enrich others at your life expense? I don't think so, unless you disagree with me, then fair enough, every individual is responsible for their own thoughts and actions.

We don't need a lot of money to live. Never use the term "to survive", as that will keep you in a poor man's mindset. Billions of dollars are wasted yearly by millions of people on flight tickets and other expenses while on temporary vacations. Where you live daily; make that the vacation place. What's the point of going somewhere for a week or two to forget the struggle you go through every day? When you return from the vacation, after a couple of days, the enjoyment of the vacation will wear out and you will go back to the same self-destructive and struggling lifestyle. Life happens in the present. Live every day as if it's your last day. Don't tell everyone about your plans/trips etc. Not everyone has your best interest in mind. Many people are good people but naïve, they cannot understand what you understand, so do what you have to do without needing validation from others.

People who retire age faster than those who continue to work. This doesn't mean that you should continue to work for corporations. What I mean is that, when you retire (you should never retire from life), you should keep engaging in activities. You should continue living uninterruptedly. Re-tire means to begin again getting tired. This is not about the etymology of the word but about how I see the word and how it sounds. Words and their meanings also age you. Words are made of low and high frequency. Use positive words, use words that fill you with joy and happiness and not words that lower your vibration, which keeps you in a defeated, destructive, lazy and a passive state of existence.

When I used to work for corporations, quite a few workers were talking about their retirement daily, they were counting the months or the years until they retired. Waiting for retirement is like waiting to die. Waiting for anything in the future robs you of the present moment. You can only live in the present moment.

***Fear of dying*** – Are we afraid of dying or afraid of living? What is death? It is an illusion. First we must analyze ourselves, are we the body or the Divine Mind/Consciousness? Knowing the answer to this question, will show us the way. If we don't know the answer or if we think we are the physical body, then we get stuck and confused in the well-crafted and elaborated trap of the 5-sense reality; the reality where we are attached to the pleasure/bodily gratifications traps.

Whether you believe or disbelieve something, if you think or talk about it enough, your consciousness will be entangled with it, therefore you will attract even things you don't want. That's why many people struggle, no matter how much they don't want to struggle or suffer; they keep the 'fear' frequency within them. Many of them (as was I years ago) have great knowledge about what to eat and drink and exercise, and yet, they are still struggling because the enemy (fear of aging and dying) is already in the house (in their mind/psyche). Before building a strong fence, we must first make sure that our house (mind) is clear of any enemies (fear, ego, apathy, lying, deception, worries, jealousy, envy, gossip, lack of mindset, resentment, grieving for a long period of time etc.) The invisible enemies just mentioned are the real enemies. There are no external enemies. So-called evil people or governments that we think are to blame, exist because of our ignorance of self. When we know our true power, nobody can control us.

## 2- UNHYGIENIC DIET - INTERNAL FILTH CAUSES AGING

Most people have in their bodies DNA from animals and other people. Meat eating ensures your DNA is intermingled with that of the animal you ate/eat. Many people who don't eat dead flesh (animal meat), consume animal and other human DNA anyway. Many foods and drinks you buy in stores have animal and human DNA in them, they are disguised in the ingredient list as "natural flavors" and or "spices". Let alone that many food purchased products have ingredients which are not listed in the ingredient list. The average person would say, "**but it's legal to disclose the ingredients on the produc**t". Anything legal or illegal can be manipulated as they see fit. They make the laws however they want, if some laws may seem like they care about you, they are there to provide a false sense of security or health.

If you go to any grocery/supermarket store (even if it's an organic one), most of the products in them are toxic. But anyways, aging will arrive if there is other DNA in you, other than your own of course. Only in the modern times people have been brainwashed to eat three meals a day. The stomach is not bigger than a fist. How much do you eat in a day? Eating more than your body needs, will stretch your stomach over a long period of time. The more stretched the stomach is, the more work for your digestive system, and the less available energy for healing the body. Even less energy for those who eat after the Sun is set. It is worse for those who eat at night, where the body must be asleep, that's when the pineal gland secretes the healing hormone called '*melatonin*'.

The synthesis and secretion of melatonin is dramatically affected by light exposure to the eyes. If you are awake when you should be asleep, you are doing the opposite of getting healed and consequently getting older, even if from the outside you may look young. Many people look young and yet they have barely any energy, they are lethargic, they seem like they are purposeless in life. And there are those who on the outside look much older than their actions; they are energetic, they exercise and also their energy when they talk is powerful and joyous. Take care of your internal body, don't waste time and money on beauty products, throw away the mirrors you have in the house.

## 3- SEXUAL INCONTINENCE - INCONTINENCE CORRUPTS THE SOUL. SEXUAL INDULGENCE ENSURES PREMATURE AGING AND DEATH

The same concept as above applies here. Having sexual intercourse with another person, will ensure you are polluted with their DNA. This may seem like nonsense to you, but the other person's body, mind, psyche is polluted from sexual interaction they had with other people. Anytime you have an orgasm, a portal opens in the astral realm. If you had sex for pleasure, to satisfy your physical senses, then through the portal, low frequency fields/entities may enter your consciousness. And if the other person is clean and healed from any sexual astral residues from their previous sexual relationships, then you will pollute them if you are not clean and/or healed.

All the sexual interactions with unhealed people whose body (mind, emotions, spirit) is polluted by astral filth, will damage the telomeres of your DNA. A damaged telomere will not regenerate which means aging and guaranteed death. But if you find (good luck, it's almost impossible) someone where sexual intercourse is genuine love from the heart and the soul for both of you, then that is fine, but only if you practice sexual alchemy. Otherwise, aging and death will surely arrive if the lifeforce (sexual secretions for both of you) is wasted as opposed to being transmuted and sent up through the spine (ladder, Sushumna channel) into the heavens a.k.a. the pineal gland, the garden of Eden (one of the interpretations).

Now, it is no longer a secret that we never die energetically. While this is true, we can be trapped in a physical body. But you may say, "so what? I like to reincarnate over and over again to help humanity".

While that's honorable, you would begin you incarnations in amnesiac state, you wouldn't remember your intentions/mission form your previous lifetime because your DNA, psyche/spirit was polluted and confused, and after passing away, Archons will be waiting for you (or not) and they could easily trick you to go through the white tunnel of light which erases your memories. That's why it is important that while alive, one must cleanse themselves physically, mentally and spiritually.

Condoms are useless. The only guaranteed way to not be polluted sexually is to not have sex with just anyone (I recommend no sex at all), no masturbations (without orgasms), as they will ensure your lifeforce energy remains stuck in the lower three chakras, no masturbation which lead to climaxing, as the portal in the astral realm opens up which will/could capture or enslave your soul or bind you to this realm.

What would the Garden of Eden be for you? A garden of Eden is perfect, you let divine nature be. If you pluck out a flower or a plant, you are disturbing the balance. Likewise, wasting your creative sexual energy disturbs the balance of your Garden Of Eden, which is your body, your nervous system, your psyche/soul. All the above three points contribute to the shortening of the telomeres in people.

## S56 TELOMERES – THE SHORTER THEY BECOME, THE FASTER YOU AGE AND VICE VERSA

During our lifetime our telomeres get shorter and shorter and this causes aging. With every cell division a small part of our telomeres is not copied and this causes them to gradually shrink. Shorter telomeres cause our DNA to become unstable and prone to express disease. The shorter our telomeres are, the older we become biologically. While the opposite is also true. The longer our telomeres, the younger our cells are biologically; and the better our health. These telomeres get damaged for the reasons mentioned in this chapter such as, bad foods, bad drinks, not enough Sun, not enough exercise, wastage of the sexual energy (which supplies the nervous system, the cells, and the whole being with life), and the BELIEF in aging.

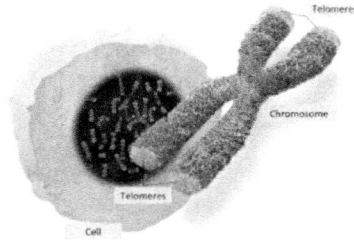

*Image is from **https://www.metabolomicclinic.com/***

The faster our cells divide, the faster our telomeres shrink. Depending on the amount of damage at a cellular level, the more damage the more cellular divisions are required. It can be easily understood then how two individuals can have the same chronological age but be in a completely different biological condition and thus biological age. Telomere length has been found to be an accurate index of the biological vs. the chronological age of an individual. The longer our telomeres, the younger our biological age while shorter telomeres are associated with higher mortality and aging related diseases. Research suggests that preserving telomeres length has the potential to prevent and treat diseases associated with aging and allow humans to increase their longevity way beyond the current theoretical maximum of 125 years.

Personally, I don't go to any doctor, mainstream or otherwise. But if you wish to know your actual age, based on your cells' health and telomeres (and not based on the calendar age), you can go and get tested. I'm not sure if it's available for the public or if you need to book an appointment. I still wouldn't go, I am my own doctor, I listen to my body and that is enough for me. But since you are not me, you have the freedom to choose. I mentioned me, to let you know that I know we can be our own doctors. Sometimes, when you go to the doctors, you return with more worries than before. You'll live longer by default if you avoid mainstream doctors. Many times people have nothing to worry about, but when they go to the doctors, they are given a so-called disease by the doctors in the form or prescription, or ideas that will become like a splinter in the mind of the patient.

## S57 AWARENESS WITHOUT EMPATHY

Anyone who strives to be on the path of awareness will find love. Any kind of love is as a result of the consequence of awareness, as a by-product, or as an unseen shadow. In this context, shadow or consequence are not words with a negative meaning but more like effect from the cause (action-reaction).

If you are someone who follows the path of love, you could find awareness as a consequence, as a by-product, as a shadow of love. These are two sides of the same coin. It's all about how you decide to take on the journey. To go from point A to point B (journey) you could begin the journey by immediately running, and eventually you may run out of breath and slow down or begin slowly and eventually you can gain momentum. In this metaphor, beginning the journey by running means that you are aware of yourself but you are going to where you want to go without taking into consideration other people, you may run over them, meaning you lack empathy.

Darkness/shadow, or trauma/tension is stored inside of us. If you acknowledge and release the stored traumatic experiences or memories, the love or the light that was always present underneath, will shine through. Someone who is on the path of awareness (assuming they're doing the inner/shadow work), they are clearing out the darkness. All that will be left is the light/love. This is about love when speaking about all sentient beings and not about intimate love toward another person. To most people, the word love just means to love intimately.

He who follows the path of love and light is not addressing the darkness, the shadow within, which doesn't go away but remains suppressed inside as dis-ease/trauma. When you address all that doesn't serve you, you will develop the ability to sense internal and external energies or frequencies. You can sense the tension/darkness or flow/love. When you practice facing your own shadow, the trauma will be dissolved. You will live in a love and empathy state of mind and heart. Everyone interprets words in their own way. In the end it's all about the life experience.

The path of love will teach you that it's all the same and connected, meaning both the light and the dark. They need to be integrated in balance. You can't always have light without darkness and vice versa. Would you live in a forest at night for the rest of your life? For the sake of the metaphor let's pretend that in the forest it will be dark forever. Would you want to live with a big bright lit bulb/light in front of your face for the rest of your life? Hopefully you get the meaning of the metaphor.

Fill yourself with love and joy. Make sure you don't forget that while you walk, your body will always leave a shadow. Life situations, experiences and self-awareness/being conscious are always present at all times, they await for you to wield the sword where you decide how your life is shaped. Be careful that you do not develop spiritual ego, or else your heart will be suppressed/tainted. Indifference will take over your life. Empathy is a must for a better world but thinking for yourself is just as crucial in becoming free.

## S58 NOW IT IS TIME TO DIE SO THAT YOU ARE BORN AGAIN

The title of this chapter may not make sense to you. It all depends on your awareness, whether you know that you are eternal or not.

You are born into this world dead (strawman, physical body, cell salt deficiency, eating/drinking), but make the best of it. You are eternal energy dressed in matter/flesh. When your flesh body expires, your wings are freed. Birth in the physical is death in the spiritual. Death in the physical is birth in the spiritual realm. Think about when you dream, you are free, you can roam wherever you want. That is your true form, your spirit is not bound by the lower realm, the physical. Enjoy this dead physical realm until you die and are reborn in the spiritual world. Do not get hung up too much on the word "dead". Just as the snake has to shade its skin, so you must shed what weighs you down. For as long as you have a physical body, you will always have to carry your body (your actual body weight) with you until the last breath, no matter how small the weight (problems, trauma etc) is.

There's a proverb that says, "when a baby is born, an ancestor returns" This means that souls reincarnate back to earth through their family lineage, if it's so, then since DNA stores information, it means the child born has information of all the life experiences of his ancestors stored in their DNA through the very beginning where life might have started from. By the look of things, the way we humans struggle to forget about past experiences of traumatic situations, it was imperative that we don't get to remember our past lives, especially if we had traumatic lives because we wouldn't be able to function well.

Forgetting doesn't necessarily mean that the information of that life isn't there, it's always there, it's just that when you're born you get hit with amnesia and forget about your previous lives. When you die you get to remember everything. Buddhist and Hindu scripture talk about attaining enlightenment so that you no longer become caught up in that cycle. To them they believe a divine spark is trapped into this material world of desire, therefore the ultimate goal is for the soul to reach its highest divinity through self-realization by attaining gnosis/knowledge of self.

The Christian Gnostic also believe that to be true, they don't believe that Jesus came to die for anyone, they believe that Christ was sent here to deliver knowledge. Within every century or so a Christ/ Buddha/Hermes or whatever name you give it, returns to remind people of their divinity. Though when it comes to orthodox Christians, I don't know whether they do believe in reincarnation or not, but Lazarus and Jesus waking up from the dead shows that they do, as a matter of fact, that's reanimation, they don't believe in reincarnation thy believe in reanimation which is bringing people back from the dead. It means to them that this life is all you have and you're here to serve and worship.

There's nothing wrong with worshipping a deity if that's for you, after all, you are both the poison and the remedy. Orthodox Christians believe that Jesus died for their sins. Their belief is the same as those of the Egyptians in some way. There's always a place waiting for you based on your character. Are you here for attaining self-realization or are you here waiting to be judged?

Reincarnation and reanimation might be two factors that influence people's beliefs and their view of the world, and they both might be real. Remember, at the end of the day it's all about bringing duality together to understand better. Just the fact that we have a physical body means that we are born in sin. Well, the word 'sin' means something to me but something else to other people. We are spirits/ energy, our physical body is dense. We are trapped in this dense realm. Do not become pessimistic by the way I use my words (also, English is my third language).

I will say what I say to get you to see things from a different angle. But even though we have a physical body we can live a beautiful and amazing life when we operate from a higher mind. At the same time I could say that there is no sin. It's all about your state of mind whether you are on the righteous path to become your own leader or whether you simply follow what the mainstream (*state/government or organized religion are both arms of the same bird*) narrative is. SIN=Separated In Nature

## S59 TRANSMUTE LEAD INTO GOLD (METAPHORICALLY)

Mankind is at its lowest it has ever been. Our current society is severely demoralized, distracted by meaningless objects and activities which serves only to keep us enslaved, away from our true selves. Man must overcome the seven planets' energies and transmute them into soul powers. Their negative forces are the seven deadly sins, which are overcome by a symbolic struggle with demons and dragons and, in turn, are transmuted into the seven cardinal virtues. This is the key to alchemy, for from the seven base metals, first spiritualized and then brought together as a secret compound, is produced the Philosophers' Stone, the purified soul.

*"In the journey of afterlife, when the lower nature has returned to brutishness, the higher struggles again to regain its spiritual estate. It ascends the seven Rings upon which sit the Seven Governors and returns to each their lower powers in this manner: Upon the first ring sits the Moon, and to it is returned the ability to increase and diminish. Upon the second ring sits Mercury, and to it are returned machinations, deceit, and craftiness.*

*Upon the third ring sits Venus, and to it are returned the lusts and passions. Upon the fourth ring sits the Sun, and to this Lord are returned ambitions. Upon the fifth ring sits Mars, and to it are returned rashness and profane boldness. Upon the sixth ring sits Jupiter, and to it are returned the sense of accumulation and riches. And upon the seventh ring sits Saturn, at the Gate of Chaos, and to it are returned falsehood and evil plotting.*

*Then, being naked of all the accumulations of the seven Rings, the soul comes to the Eighth Sphere, namely, the ring of the fixed stars. Here, freed of all illusion, it dwells in the Light and sings praises to the Father in a voice which only the pure of spirit may understand. Behold, O Hermes, there is a great mystery in the Eighth Sphere, for the Milky Way is the seed-ground of souls, and from it they drop into the Rings, and to the Milky Way they return again from the wheels of Saturn. But some cannot climb the seven-ranged ladder of the Rings. So they wander in darkness below and are swept into eternity with the illusion of sense and earthiness.* - Manly P. Hall

The rings (at least one side of the truth) are the seven chakra wheels or the energetic centers. Those chakras are Root, Sacral, Solar Plexus, Heart, Throat, Third Eye and the Crown. These chakras, although not visible, are located within the body from the bottom of the spine, and all the way to the top of the head. There are many more chakras, but taking care of the main seven is a priority. That which is above (the seven planets) correspond to the seven chakras in us. If planets (luminaries) didn't exist, we could not exist either. J.J. & TAMO, in their book, "**The Path to Greatness**" say:

> "Your energy centers are your inner suns or chakras. These inner suns are whirls of energy in the form of a torus which connects consciousness with existence. There is only one consciousness, the complete, absolute one that we all are part of. The word chakra means whirl of wheel because these energy centers spin in circles like a wheel. These energy centers cannot be seen with the naked eye, but they can be seen/felt spiritually when you attune yourself to the spiritual void, when you vibrate very high in frequency you can see (with your third eye) things you cannot see with your physical eyes. The more you associate with your inner suns, the more you end up in the flow of your natural course or life path".

When your energy centers begin to open or unblock, your digestive fire is stronger, your mind becomes clearer, your intentions become stronger and you feel loved and you will emit love back to the world. Your heart is your central sun. Your heart is the fourth energy center/chakra whether you begin counting from the bottom or the top. Your heart is in the middle, there are three chakras (or inner suns) above the heart chakra and three below, a total of 7 major chakras. Starting from the bottom, the order of the inner suns are: the Root, Sacral, Solar Plexus, Heart, Throat, Third Eye and Crown. Chakras have their own individual colors which are in agreement/accordance/unity with the basic colors of the spectrum of sunlight.

These energy centers (chakras or inner suns) are on the exact location of the glands in the human body which determine all the hormonal functions as well as functioning of all the vital organs. We are much more complicated than we think we are. We are not just our physical body.

Technically, we have a body but we are not it. It is imperative to balance the inner suns. In some books or online you may have read/heard "activating the chakras". Without activated chakras we wouldn't be able to exist. I'm sure the authors meant "balancing the chakras". We all have them since birth, but with time our body ends up in disharmony from a myriad of external poisons/influences. It is very important that what you think, say and do daily, must be positive for an optimal healthy existence.

Everything you hear and see affects your glands, organs, chakras and everything that makes you, "YOU". Your body receives sunlight through the eyes at most. The chakras, sunlight, colors and the functioning of the vital organs interconnect in one union which gives life. These energy centers play a crucial role in our physical, emotional, and spiritual well-being. Understanding their significance can help you identify any blockages or imbalances, allowing you to take steps towards healing and balance.

(a) **ROOT** chakra deals with Survival. This chakra is blocked by fear.

(b) **SACRAL** chakra deals with Pleasure; it is blocked by guilt.

(c) **SOLAR PLEXUS** chakra deals with Willpower; it is blocked by shame.

(d) **HEART** chakra deals with Love and it is blocked by grief.

(e) **THROAT** chakra deals with Truth; it is blocked by lies.

(f) **THIRD EYE** chakra deals with Insight and it is blocked by illusion.

(g) **CROWN** chakra deals with Cosmic Energy; it is blocked by ego".

As you can see from the above points, a – g, all seven chakras must be balanced if we want to operate in an optimal healthy state. Reference to the above point any time you have a problem in you, and work based on that problem/need. Since we are surrounded with all kinds of people, it seems very difficult to make a big improvement in life. Thereby, "solitude" is advisable. Only in solitude, will we be able to hear our innermost true voice. If we spend our time gossiping about others, or listening to many people's opinions daily, we will not have time to converse with our inner self, our true authentic being. It's how we transmute darkness into light, unconsciousness to self-awareness, lead to gold; through discipline, determination and will power.

> "At death the material body of man is returned to the elements
> from which it came, and the invisible divine man ascends to
> the source from whence he came, namely the Eighth Sphere.
> The evil passes to the dwelling place of the demon, and the
> senses, feelings, desires, and body passions return to their

*source, namely the Seven Governors, whose natures in the lower man destroys but in the invisible spiritual man gives life.*
**-Manly P Hall**

# PART FOUR

## SEXUAL ENERGY - CONTINENCE

# SEXUALITY

"Chastity, therefore, is both a discipline and a state of being. It purifies the astral body, enabling the soul to resonate with the frequency of the white dragon consciousness. This consciousness in not merely an abstract ideal but a living reality within the astral light, a force that empowers the soul to transcend the lower dimensions of the titanic existence and embrace the infinite. In this state, the initiate achieves gnosis - not through external knowledge but through an inward experience that arises when the soul, body, and spirit are aligned"
 – J.J. The Internal Dragon: The Art of Self–Mastery

## 560 SPIRITUAL WARWFARE THROUGH LUST

We live in a pleasure/indulgence-based society. For the average person, pleasure of the senses is the ultimate good and that is false. The gratification of the bodily pleasures has choked this society to death. Death is not supposed to exist, unfortunately, death exists because life force is wasted continually through the 5-sense bodily gratifications through poison foods, drinks, content and through the wastage of the creative sexual energy. Lust is demonic consciousness or a low frequency thought pattern.

The average (most men and women, but especially men) people, squander their creative potential/energy through conventional sexual interactions, masturbation and orgasms. Sex is not a plaything as the dark magicians (behind the curtain controllers) want people to believe. Sexual energy is your savior if you use it wisely by transmuting it , or your tomb if you use it for gratification purposes. Let alone that when you have an orgasm, portals from the astral world open up where interdimensional beings of low vibrational frequency sneak into your consciousness.

Most people are possessed and they don't even know it. Most people believe that what they think, are their thoughts. Interdimensional beings or microscopic parasites mimic human thoughts and behavior. The world is loaded up with false information that orgasms, sex and masturbations are healthy. They are not, they are early death behavior. If you are still controlled by lust I can't expect you to immediately understand, but at least consider the possibility that everything you have been taught about sexual energy is wrong with the purpose to control your life and the lives of your children. When I speak about the sexual energy subject to people in real life or online, sometimes I'm called a sex hater or a woman hater. Obviously, these people's consciousness resides in hell (bottom half of the body where the gut, lower three chakras are, and their genitals). We cannot think clearly when our consciousness is not of a high faculty level. Years ago, I too, thought that some people were women haters when they were talking to me about this stuff where at that time I had no clue about.

At that time all I knew was to have sex, masturbate and feed my belly with junk food and drinks, which made me be classified lower than the average man, pretty much an animal (without talking down to the actual animals). Actually animals are better than many humans. Animals don't procreate any time they feel. They procreate in season. Only humans with so-called 'higher mind' procreate anytime they feel like, or unconscious pregnancies as a result of being drunk or driven by lust.

> "The ejaculation and subsequent loss of seminal fluids is highly taxing process on the organism. In some species, it even marks the end of life"  *The SR Manuscript by Edward Green*

Those entities will latch into your body and feed off your energy every time you masturbate, have sex and climaxes. Pleasure doesn't mean truth, but illusion. Have you ever heard the name "Asmodeus"? He or she is the demon of lust. Just as there are presidents/controllers in government in this physical reality, so are there controllers in the astral realm. Asmodeus is the prince of lust, which is fed constantly by humanity's wasted sexual energy through porn, conventional sex etc. To read about Asmodeus and other sexual subjects, check out these two books:

***TO BE REBORN*** by Tamo A. Replica
***THE INTERNAL DRAGON*** by J.J

In the same book as the one mentioned above by Tamo A. Replica, Tamo writes,

> "The normalization of porn is an agenda to turn men into docile zombies, weak and in their animal consciousness. This is not to put down the animals as animals are perfect for what they have been programmed to do and be. Animal consciousness means that those men who are controlled by lust, don't have a higher consciousness, they don't have the rational higher state of mind that only humans' brains are equipped with. Animals function by instinct. As a man if you operate from an animalistic basic instinct, your life is forfeited. The real agenda should be to retain the semen, to refuse to spill the seed or

the life force. Doing that, will unleash Divine masculinity in the world and it will ignite men's spiritual consciousness. Man is half man and half beast. All the goodness [lifeforce] given to us by default, is wasted carelessly. We have a mind to think for ourselves therefore the gift should be used as a catalyst for a higher purpose of living and not wasting it to the point that binds us into physical, mental, emotional and spiritual shackles".

The real warfare is spiritual, real warfare is unseen, real warfare happens in the mind (your mind, **micro**cosmically) and in the GREAT MIND (**macro**cosmically). You cannot be at war if you are not conflicted internally. When our thoughts, emotions and actions are not harmonized, our internal conflict makes us easier to be manipulated, it causes ego to defend itself by rejecting any information that disproves our unconscious/low awareness attitude. Lust is number one in the list of how to control a species. See your sexual energy as if it was your bank account, which money is energy by the way. Every time you mismanage your sexual energy, meaning when you waste it as opposed to transmute it internally through creative endeavors, your being's energy or LIGHT is diminished. When light/life force is diminished it means that early death is a certainty.

## S61 THERE ARE BARELY ANY INTELLIGENT CREATIVE PEOPLE IN THE MODERN TIMES.

The greatest achievements in human history–from architectural marvels to technological breakthroughs–were accomplished by individuals who learned to harness and direct their creative sexual energy toward meaningful pursuits such as inventions, craftsmanship, art (painting, drawing), writing, singing etc. You don't have to be acknowledged officially to be called a creative person, like singers, inventors etc. You can be creative in the comfort of your home. You shouldn't need any external validation for anything that you accomplish in life. Modern architectural buildings are soulless, movies are immoral, song lyrics full of low frequency cursing/swearing words.

Your sexual energy, when properly channeled through creativity and not by wasting it through the exit channel a.k.a ejaculating your semen or menstruating by wasting your life force (blood and eggs), becomes the fuel for innovation, artistic expression, and personal transformation, creating a positive ripple effect that extends far beyond your individual existence. We don't know what we don't know, and what we know may be valid just for the present.

## S62 TAMPONS CAUSE CANCER AND OTHER PROBLEMS

Conventional tampons contain GMO-filled cotton, with plastic fibers, chlorinated wood pulp, glyphosate and many other toxic chemicals. While the tampons stay in the body for hours, the chemicals leach into the system. Anything toxic which leeches into the system, acidifies and pollutes the blood, weakens the nervous system and consequently causes premature aging and death. This system provides products that make it comfortable for people to use.

Comfort is a disease. We cannot grow in a comfortable environment. Comfort brings laziness and passiveness where we don't act when we need to act the most. Laziness destroys creativity and life in general. Tampons and other beauty products have been invented to destroy women's endocrine system. The feminine creates life; women have been suppressed for far too long, it is time that you take care of your health. You don't need anything this system provides; products which are designed to lower your frequency, to destroy your body and mind, and to capture your soul in a never-ending cycle of reincarnation.

## S63 SEXUAL CONTINENCE (not wasting your sexual fluids/secretions) – SEMEN RETENTION

Most people would blame money, bad food/drinks, materialism, news channels, wars, etc. for the suffering in the world but all these are results of the main problem which is 'sexual incontinence'. There was a reason why giving certain knowledge to people was dangerous. Creative sexual energy/knowledge can be dangerous in the hands of those (meaning the masses, the average human) who will profane it. People nowadays are exposed to sexualization from a very young age. Their sexual glands, by the time they reach mid-twenties are irritated and depleted.

Many men are emasculated simply by abusing sexual energy. Sexual energy must be channeled to achieve a higher state of consciousness, to walk the path of Light. Ejaculating (*or wasting any secretion – including the 'blood end eggs', if you are a woman*) is dark magic. This may be new to you, but that's what it is, black magic. The dark magicians spill their sexual fluid, while the white magician contains it and transmutes it to Divine Consciousness.

**1$^{ST}$ STEP** – As a first step to semen retention, before ejaculating, one could simply press hard between anus and the scrotum so that the semen doesn't get expelled/ejaculated. Some semen will still escape through the urine, some of the semen will be redirected into the bladder. With this, you will still lose some of your life force, but at least it is something to begin so that you train yourself to go to an intermediate level where you don't ejaculate anymore.

**2$^{ND}$ STEP** – No sexual intercourse whatsoever, no matter how hungry the husband or the wife is. Sex for pleasure is immoral anyway. Being hungry for it, means that your consciousness or energy is concentrated on the lower three chakras of the body, that's where the so-called black magicians/controllers want people at. They don't want people's energy to rise above the 3$^{rd}$ chakra (solar plexus); the 4$^{th}$ chakra is the heart. It is time to make decisions. Controlling hunger and lust are the two major tests. It is important to control what you eat and also what information you put in your mind, because any low frequency content or food/drinks that you feed yourself with, will acidify your body. A person with an acidic blood, will be prone to fall to hunger and lust; these two are low consciousness states.

Many men fail in retaining indefinitely because they think that they just retain their seed and that's it. Many of them waste their life force (semen which contains phosphorus, the most important mineral for brain's intelligence) while asleep, through wet dreams. If you are a man (who practices semen retention) reading this, you may have read somewhere that when you have wet dreams, it is not a relapse. That is false, it is a 100% a relapse. No such a thing as *"extra semen that is not needed, will be ejaculated through wet dreams"*. Your body produces constantly semen, but it contains your life force needed to supply your whole being constantly. See, the big problem is not having a wet dream here and there (which is a problem nonetheless), the big problem is that even if you have a wet dream, it must not be more than once in 74 days (the duration needed for full spermatozoa maturity). You cannot possibly know how many times in one month you have a wet dream. Most of the time, people can't remember their dreams.

Having wet dreams simply means "wasted and untransmuted

sexual energy". Sexual energy is very powerful, and energy needs to flow. Transmuting your sexual energy means raising your energy up the spine and onto the head/pineal gland through meditation, lifting weights, and doing any creative activities. If the accumulated energy is not transmuted, it will have to flow somewhere, in this case, it will be ejected through your penis at night, or even while awake through just pre-ejaculations in small amounts, assuming you are aroused somehow. Any amount of ejaculation, no matter how small, it is detrimental. But of course, the more you ejaculate, the worse. The same applies to women, you too will lose secretions/life force if you don't transmute the energy.

## S64 SEXUAL INTERCOURSE DURING GESTATION ENSURES THE BIRTH OF AVERAGE CHILDREN – IT LOWERS INTELLIGENCE

The dangers of sexual intercourse during the gestation period and after the infant's birth, have been prevalent for a long time, hence the lower IQ of the world's population since the introduction of pornography and sexualization in general, especially in the internet era of the last decades.

What most men and women don't know, is that they should not have any sexual interaction (including masturbation, fellatio or orgasms) during gestation and after the baby is born, until the baby reaches 2.5-3 years of age (make it a habit to not use the word "old" when mentioning someone's age, whether they are babies, children or adults).

This subtitle may anger or trigger in a negative way some people. Almost, if not all parents would think their children are intelligent, even though they are average. How do we judge the level of intelligence? All we can do is compare anyone or anything according to our current knowledge and wisdom. I have a question for you (and for myself, which I know the answer),

**"Are you more intelligent than 5 years ago, or are you less stupid than 5 years ago?"**

We have been conditioned to compare in a way which makes us feel good, in a positive way. How about we compare differently so that we leave room for improvement? Personally, every rising/morning that I get up from travelling in the astral world, or the world beyond, I say to myself, *"I know nothing"*. What this does, it empowers me to learn much more than before, it catapults me to farther and greater horizons. If we say, "We know everything" or even if we think "we know everything", it puts us in the back seat, it makes us lazy. What "lazy" means for you, means something else to someone else. If you read a book a month, it may seem intelligence compared to reading ZERO books, but how about we compare it with a hypothetical scenario where we read 10 books a month? The point is that to obtain intelligence, we must aim to take 2-3 steps in life so that we can walk one full step.

So, sometimes saying a phrase in a negative way, such as the example, "I know nothing", can become a positive statement. The book example was simply to get you to compare hypothetical scenarios. A lot of people don't read books, they simply read articles online, or watch YouTube videos. There are also others who obtain knowledge in the silence of their mind, through deep meditation. Truth arrives from different angles. You pick whichever you think is best for you.

Schlapp studied hundreds of cases of cretins born of normal parents and his conclusion was that a prenatal injury to the thyroid and other glands of the embryo by an endocrine disturbance in the mother was the basic cause of such conditions.

Max Gustav Schlapp (1869-1928) professor of the New York Post-Graduate Medical School has this to say about average children born from unconscious parents:

"Glandular depletion of the mother during gestation is the basic cause of the production of cretins and idiots, when there is no direct hereditary causation. It is clear that such "glandular depletion" can result from the excessive withdrawal of phosphatides from the mother's blood as a result of sexual intercourse during pregnancy, which also tends to produce endocrine dysfunction in the form of glandular hyper-and-hypo activities".

He goes on to say: "The development of the embryonic brain is largely determined by chemical conditions affecting the brain of the embryo during its development. Thus, a lack of iodine in the diet of a pregnant mother may cause underdevelopment of the thyroid gland and brain of the embryo, resulting in an idiot. On the other hand, an abundance of iodine will lead to the birth of a child with a superior brain".

Men who ejaculate, also lose phosphorus, which is the main building block for intelligence. The unintelligence of the children is directly attributed to the bad diet and sexual intercourse during gestation by the parents. Not only this, but also the amount of times a man (or a woman) ejaculates before the spermatozoa reaches full maturity at day 70-74. In other words, a man must not ejaculate for at least 74 days before having a chance at conceiving an above average child.

Decades ago, before the internet era began, those parents had sexual intercourse while the future mother was pregnant also. But there are more average children born in the internet era than before, because of the normalization of porn or sexualization in general. Before, parents were busy with other useful things, but nowadays, while on the internet, it is almost impossible to not see at least a post a day without sexualization, be it a video clip, or writing (posts, messages, articles etc.).

You cannot even go to the mall with kids anymore, many stores sexualize everything where they have almost naked women's posters for everyone that walks by to see, such as in clothing or lingerie stores. A lot of children see this; even if the children don't know anything about sex, the images of the posters (or soft sexualization on Tv ads, cartoons, TV shows etc.) penetrate their subconscious mind, a little at a time and eventually all sorts of immoralities are seen as normal by the child when is grown up. Protect the children at all costs.

"Many ills and great suffering are directly traceable to excessive sexual intercourse during the non-pregnant state; and sexual intercourse during pregnancy is responsible for an almost endless list of physical and mental defects, ranging all the way from color-blindness to idiocy; and the number of physical and mental defectiveness, due to this cause, is rapidly increasing from year to year. It is also responsible for universal unhappiness among married women who know instinctively that it is harmful". - Thurston: *Thurston's Philosophy of Marriage Maternal chastity, before and after conception, leads to opposite results.*

Eames, in *"The Principle of Eugenics"* describes an experiment in which the reproductive cells of an individual were microscopically examined after a period of dissipation, and again, after one of continence. In the latter case they were larger and more vital than in the former. The author remarks that children born from devitalized reproductive cells would be physically and mentally inferior to those born from the others.

Another doctor/author, Dr. Raymond Bernard, has this to say in page 129 of his book *Creation of the Superman*, about the dangers of having sex before and while in pregnancy/gestation:

> "The embryo is a condensation of the maternal blood; and for an embryonic superman to be formed, super-blood is required. The blood of the mother is enriched and vitalized chiefly by her glandular secretions, particularly by those of the sex glands. There exists a very intimate relationship between the maternal genital secretions, or hormones, and the growing brain of the fetus. On this account, excessive sexual intercourse, previous to conception and during gestation, by draining the mother's blood of genital secretions which are otherwise lymphatically absorbed and used for the construction of embryonic brain-tissue (since these secretions are very rich in phosphorus, the principal element required for the formation of nerve-cells), results in the birth of a physically and mentally subnormal child".

Even if the parents don't have sex in the gestation period; if the father (or the mother) waste their sexual glands' secretions (hormones, phosphorus, stem cells etc.) through other ways (masturbation, fellatio etc.) other than through sexual intercourse, the child may still be subnormal. The doctors' quotes speak of the dangers of sexual intercourse, but the point is to not waste the life force (secretions from both parents' sexual glands, especially the mother), which they are wasted also through fellatios, masturbations, orgasms and arousal in general.

Many words have lost their meaning. The truth has been watered down. Political correctness has created a generation (young and adults) of people who are happy to just exist, by feeling good just to be average. One word that has been watered down is the word "average". Many people (half of those, I personally know them) think that being average is not bad. Why is that? That's because many behaviors, self-esteem, character building, and discipline have been watered down to where people think and believe that to be average is to be intelligent. I have met quite a few people who called me intelligent just because I was explaining to them elementary stuff (about thinking for yourself, how the system works etc.). I'm far from being intelligent. One thing is certain, that I am less stupid than the day before.

When we think we are intelligent, not only do we learn less, but we may develop a brutal ego, we may become megalomaniacs or narcissists. My recommendation to everyone is that we must humble ourselves, we must remind ourselves that we are not better than anyone else, and nobody is better than ourselves. But at the same time, we must also learn to discern, live a life where our choices derive from self-awareness and not through carelessness.

Max G. Schlapp, Dr. Raymond W. Bernard, Professor Hilton Hotema, Professor Arnol Ehret and many others from decades ago (before the so-called modern medicine took over), were very knowledgeable about human anatomy/physiology in detail. They were homeopathists, they were against synthetic chemicals/medicine and definitely against chopping off (surgery) the body. We are nature, and we can only be healed by nature (herbal medicine, Sun, grounding etc.). Unfortunately, humanity has been conditioned to think that we are at the height of medicine. What this does, is, it makes many people ignore knowledge from decades ago or from 100, or thousands of years ago.

There is no new knowledge, what we think is new, is simply rediscovered knowledge. Many times I attempted to get people to read certain books from 100 years ago, they didn't even touch the books, because it was knowledge from a long time ago. There is a very thin line between closed and open mindedness.

## S65 PLACENTA – DOES IT COME FROM THE FATHER OR FROM THE MOTHER?

The building blocks for creating a child are provided by both parents. One provides the materials, and the other has the tools and the house to build the miracle. The word "placenta" in Greek means "cake". The placenta is the original birthday cake and that's the thing that gets celebrated. We celebrate the cake, not the baby. As long as we keep celebrating the birthday cake/the placenta, we will always be punished because that material dies within a couple of days and that biology becomes a decedent estate that requires a trust, a trust fund, fiduciaries to manage it.

The decedent estate requires administrative process by the courts. This is related to the STRAWMAN, the 2D fictional birth certificated character that exists only on the CROWN copyrighted paper/plastic legal documents that you have been carrying all life until now, believing that you are the STRAWMAN, but you are NOT. The placenta is an extension of the baby. When the baby is born, the hospital keeps the placenta without your consent. The placenta belongs to the baby, you must ask for it after the baby is born, do not leave the maternity ward until they give you the placenta. If you don't ask for it, they will sell it for 30,000 – 100,000 dollars.

With the DNA of the placenta of your baby, they can clone another being. And if not, they use the placenta's stem cells for experiments and who knows what else.

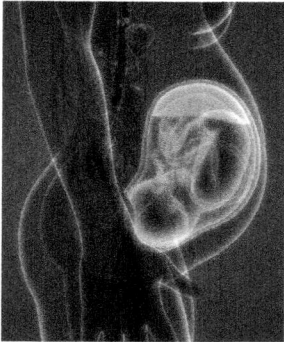

The placenta comes from the father, the genetic material that forms the placenta comes/is inherited from the father. But the mother is needed to house the placenta, after it is being created. Father's genes are responsible for creating the placenta. Mother's genes are responsible for the creation of the embryo. When a mother gives birth to a baby, is the placenta or the uterus being expelled? The placenta of course. The placenta belongs to the baby, it is an extension of the fetus/baby. The placenta provided the essential nutrients that babies need to survive. Placenta's health is crucial in the development of a healthy baby. In this case, what the mother drinks and eats is very important., Not just food or drinks consumption but also mental and emotional health is important.

When the placenta comes out, it brings with it also the uterine lining with it. The uterus lining (beside the liver which regenerates continually) regenerates and is expelled continually/repeatedly. Isn't it amazing? The human body is a marvel. It is created to perfection. If there is physical, emotional or mental disease, it is because the human mind creates suffering, from too much overanalyzing. The embryo provides everything the placenta needs to be created. But of course, the mother's blood/DNA is needed for compatibility, so is the father's DNA.

The embryo tricks the mother's body into not rejecting the embryo. I could go on and on with different examples about the importance of both the mother and the father but I won't. There is no point, you decide for yourself if both genders are needed or not. We live in times where there are many agendas and so-called studies (false studies), whose sole intention is to confuse both genders and people in general, or lure men and women into arguing with each other about which gender is more important. If you argue with each other, they get you by the balls and by the non-balls.

It's all about Yin/Yang energy. What one gender/parent lacks, is compensated by the other. Together both genders complement each other. Stop fighting, it's how the controllers win by pinning us against each other, by causing us to create our hell and their paradise. Even a simple device plugging on the wall tells us the importance of male and female interaction and acceptance. Do you think that the wall outlet is arguing with your phone's charging plug as to which one is giving life to your cell phone? Of course not, they operate as they should.

Just as the semen/sexual energy and the egg operate as they should. It's the human mind that creates the chaos in the world. Way back in time, people operated from their heart center, they lived in peace, they were connected with nature/creation. When societies began using the mind, being predominantly logical, that's when mankind began decaying rapidly. And also the degeneration of our society accelerated fast when people began having sex for pleasure and not just for procreating.

The father's genes make up the majority of the placenta, but it also needs components from the mother, otherwise the placenta would not stick to the uterus or it wouldn't form properly. Another reason as to why miscarriages happen is because parents have sex while the mother is in gestation period.

Every time you (men vs women) argue with each other, your enlightenment path ends up being farther away. It is pointless arguing who (the mother or the father) created the placenta, who created the legs, eyes, brain etc. Children don't come from you but THROUGH you. For as long as you point fingers at external beings, you have a long way to go. Both women and men have strengths and weaknesses. Mothers and fathers complement each other when they operate from a place of self-awareness, critical thinking mindset and from an open heart. I'll tell you why the arguing happens. Almost everyone, if not everyone, has had a bad relationship.

Many people hold on to grudges and resentments. Many people have narcissistic tendencies. Memories of the past may cause you to bleed on someone in the present who didn't cut/hurt you. Emotions are beautiful but only when you have them under control and are not controlled by them. Arguing, especially in regards to gender, is because people strongly identify with their gender to the point they dismiss the other gender, without realizing that both genders are equally important and needed to have a peaceful society.

Understand that if someone hurt you in the past, they were not being their true self at that time. It does not mean that they are the same even now. Everyone grows/progresses, no matter how slow. But if someone is indeed creating a negative energetic environment for you, then feel free to choose a different environment. But before you do that, make sure that you are not the one that is causing the negativity as a result of your past bad memories or egoistic/selfish state of existence. I cannot tell you who you are, only you know yourself. The moment we stop lying to ourselves is the moment we begin living and providing an environment for a happy and joyous life for ourselves and others.

## S66 CHASTITY OR CELIBACY IS THE HIGHEST DISCIPLINE ONE CAN ATTAIN

When you retain your seed (or your secretions if you are a woman) through celibacy or chastity plus sexual alchemy a.k.a. tantric sex without wasting any secretions externally, you liberate the soul. It is not a secret anymore that the soul never dies, and that it can never be destroyed, but it can be enslaved through the 5-sense (sight, touch, hearing, smell and taste) gratification trap.

**S i g h t** – materialism, judging based on looks, pornography, immoral content, blood/wars, cheating etc. on TV, TV shows, magazines and social media. – All these enslave the soul.

**H e a r I n g** – Gossiping is rampant in our society. The more time you spend with a lot of people, the more nonsense you will hear. Even if some things are useful, adding more to your brain is not necessarily good. The ears must go on vacation more often. But also songs of low frequency are very harmful. In the last two decades many song talk about cheating, killing, blood and they use a lot of low frequency words which keeps your vibration down/low.

**S m e l l** – Fragrance, deodorant, lipsticks, perfume, hair gel, or anything else that we use, are very damaging to our endocrine system.

**T a s t e** – food and drinks are the main causes that cause one to become physically sick, and mentally of course. This system is abundant of poisons created to enslave you. Consume only raw natural food that comes from the ground. Everything is natural, but in this case I'm speaking of the good natural food which is created to be properly assimilated by your body. Fluoride is also natural, but that doesn't mean it is good for you.

**T o u c h** – If one has seen or heard images/sound of sexualization content, will fall easily into the trap of touching another person, a person that may be some kind of sexual attraction or not yet.

All the 5 senses influence each other. To purify the soul, one must feed all senses with positivity and beauty, with the understanding that what you feed your five senses doesn't feed your ego, lust, selfishness, greed, etc. Whether you have conventional sex, masturbate, fellatio or orgasm, you lose vital force/energy through secretions anyway and energetically. Before any part of your body (including sexual secretions) materializes, it exists first in the energetic form in the astral body, the non-physical so-called vessel.

Through a chaste or celibate life, everything good is multiplied in energy and feeling. The natural food you eat will be enjoyed much more. You appreciate nature and everything in it. Many people interact with nature, but in an unconscious state and that's a pity. Here's an example, two friends have to go somewhere, but they have to walk through a park to get to where they need to go. These friends, during their walk through the park/woods, talk about electronic gadgets, politics, celebrities, actors, singers, porn/sex etc. Their soul was in much need to interact with nature. Interacting with nature means looking at the grass, trees, squirrels; hear the sound of the breeze, the chirping of the birds, touching and hugging the trees or plants, observing the ant colony, the bees hopping from one flower to another.

There is a whole world just within that hypothetical scenario/ park and in reality, and yet it was missed by the boys because they were engaging in useless conversations. Hypothetical or not, we all at some point have missed a lot of natural beauty just because we were focused on anything but nature. Many times we are lost in our thoughts, we make up scenarios for situations that haven't arrived yet, and it is not guaranteed they will happen/arrive. The point is to let go of the overthinking mind and focus on the moment, that's when magic happens, that's why meditation is very important to stay away from the 5 thieves (5 senses), which rob us of our soul.

*"Chastity, therefore, is both a discipline and a state of being. It purifies the*

*astral body, enabling the soul to resonate with the frequency of the white dragon consciousness. This consciousness is not merely an abstract ideal but a living reality within the astral light, a force that empowers the soul to transcend the lower dimensions of the titanic existence and embrace the infinite. In this state, the initiate achieves gnosis – not through external knowledge but through an inward experience that arises when the soul, body, and spirit are aligned"* - J.J. ***The Internal Dragon: The Art of Self-Mastery***

When you have sex, you use all 5 senses, therefore you are contained within the 5-sense reality. It's one thing to reciprocate love and another to have sex just to satisfy the bodily pleasures. Love is made from the soul. Sex is simply to satisfy the senses or procreate, which is the animalistic lower form of procreation, with the highest form of procreation being PARTHENOGENESIS or virgin birth. Somewhere in this book I recommended another book which speaks about how to achieve a parthenogenetic birth, meaning how to procreate without sexual intercourse.

You will never see a utopian society unless one frees their soul from being trapped in the five-sense reality. I must tell you not to be confused with the utopian version that the government is trying to sell us. You know, they advertise the new sustainable life with a universal income for everyone where nobody needs to work, They want everyone to be 100% a slave, with zero free will. That's a fake utopian society that they are trying to create. That would be a dystopian society for us, but utopian to them.

Picture yourself at work where the boss is giving everyone 10 dollars more per hour, whether someone is a hard worker or lazy. Is that good or bad? The end goal for you should be to never work again for anyone, and definitely not for a corporation. But to attain what you are deserving by default, you must cultivate virtues, it takes effort but it is doable. It is more rewarding when you work on yourself. A cat won't chase a mouse that is not moving.

A cat will work to catch its prey. Likewise, human beings feel more rewarded when they work for what they desire. If someone gives you $1,000, but you also have another $1,000 that you worked hard for; which one would you spend faster without critically thinking and which one will you think twice before you spend it on useful or useless things?

## S67 PARTHENOGENESIS – DIVINE ALCHEMY BIRTH WITHOUT SEXUAL INTERCOURSE

Procreating through the ordinary way (through sexual intercourse), doesn't mean that it's not divine, it simply is the lowest form of divine unity, it is the animalistic way of procreating. UNLESS, you have mastered tantric sex where you make love with the opposite gender and then she gets pregnant, but without you ejaculating, and without her excreting any vital fluids externally.

What I just described is almost impossible for the fact that all people are unhealed one way or another. Therefore, the best choice/ way to procreate is the one without sexual intercourse. But just as you read in this chapter, chastity and a 100% hygienic diet are a must, or else the electromagnetism won't be strong enough to fertilize the woman's eggs.

The woman holds the necessary materials for the formation of the offspring. The role of the man is in awakening the formative powers possessed by the woman, which lie dormant in the female product.

Blondel, in *The Power of the Mother's Imagination over the Foetus* wrote: "All parts of the foetus/fetus, both small and great, internal and external, are in the ovum. And though some appear later than others, yet they have been co-existing, and have had their beginning at the same time – as an acorn, which, even before it be set in the ground, does contain an epitome of the oak, with all its roots, branches and leaves".

Researches and scientific investigations have proven that spermatozoa add no germinal material to the egg they fertilize, but act as catalytic agents, chemically stimulating them to cell-division and embryonic growth. Whether the spermatozoa adds germinal material to the egg or whether the male simply awakens the egg and the process for the conception of the fetus makes no difference, male is needed. Please, don't fall for a certain agenda who uses this subject (parthenogenesis) to put down males. Any agenda, whether it is against the man or the woman, on the surface it seems like they (whoever they may be) care about one gender or the other. 'THEY' don't care, all the agendas are there to distract people, to pin people, in this case men and women, against each other.

I already mentioned in this book, Dr. Raymond W. Bernard's

book *'Creation of the Superman'*. He explains this subject (plus how to stop menstruating and menopause) better than me. Depending on each individual's state of knowledge/wisdom of themselves and life in general, this subject may be interesting to some and nonsense to others. That is perfectly fine. Certain knowledge is embraced by those who seek it and rejected by those who are just happy to exist.

# PART FIVE

## A LITTLE BIT OF THIS & A LITTLE BIT OF THAT

## La Petite Mort – Little Death

"When you achieve that intense excitement or orgasm, your consciousness is killed (or you lose your consciousness) for a few seconds, which in turn takes off a chunk out of your life. Your lifespan gets shortened. These moments of climax bind you in the 3D physical realm. Every time you have an orgasm, your chance to leave your body at will so as to never reincarnate again with amnesia, is diminished. Naturally, we are connected with a filmy connecting link or a silver cord to the astral world, our real home [have in mind the adage "As Above So Below]. The more you orgasm, the further away will your chance to go 'Home' be. But when you practice continence of your fluids [semen for men and ovum for women], i.e. not spilling your sexual fluids, the stronger the link becomes between your real self/astral body and the 'Source' where you're originally from in the astral world/Home. Conquer your drug addiction [climax/orgasm] if you don't want to keep reincarnating with amnesia over and over again in a 3D reality of wars, famine, suffering, materialism etc."

— Tamo A. Replica, TO BE REBORN, p.122

I knew a cat boxer. Nobody else was brave enough to fight with him. Of course I'm joking. They defend you with their unseen energy. In ancient times cats were revered as their (ancients') protectors in the astral realm. You may be someone who prefers dogs to cats but if you can, I suggest you look into adopting a cat. Compared to dogs, cats can see at night (astral entities), just as reptilians and any other nocturnal animals do. If you have kids and cats at home, chances are that kids usually bother and chase them. When/if there is an invisible entity in the house, the cat will go and chase it away if the entity is of a negative energy, or communicate with it if the entity is of a positive energy. Many times the cats sleep with the owner or sit on the couch or other places for a while.

Don't move the cat away from where they're sitting. Cats can not only sense other entities in the house, but they can also sense any problem in your auric field. Beside your whole being's aura, each of your organs also have their own auric field. When an organ is damaged (even though you may not feel any pain yet) the cat can heal it (until a certain point, you must do your job too, in healing yourself). That's why many times, cats keep you company, they sense the low vibrational frequency of any organs you may have problems with, at least that's one of the reasons. If you think this is a far-fetched theory, I urge you to rethink.

Realize that there is only energy in creation. What we see with our eyes is simply an illusion or a manifestation of the true existence which is 'Consciousness' or 'energy field'. Another way to repel negative entities is to light a candle at night before you go to sleep. Light overpowers darkness. The candle, not only that it will repel negative entities, but it is also useful in helping the activation of your pineal gland.

Before you meditate, for a few minutes look at the candle flame and think/visualize that the energy from it is entering your pineal gland between your eyebrows. The negative entities could be deceased people that were attached to your house, assuming you purchased a used house. The entity that was living there when he/she was alive, was attached to that house or any other reasons that are tied to that house. That spirit is confused, so the only place that it is familiar to is the house. Do not be scared. You can repel it away with candlelight, mental mantras such as the one below:

*"I (insert your name) ask that every negative energetic work, aggressors and entities not coming from the Light, be addressed to my human being, or any member of my family. If you (you are directing your words at the entity) are here with a loving intention, then you are welcomed to guide me in my spiritual journey. Otherwise, if your intention is to harm or manipulate my consciousness in any way to my disadvantage, then you must immediately leave".*

Practice mentally this decree before meditating, when you wake up or anywhere or any time you feel heavy of thoughts or concerns or anything that doesn't align with love/divinity. When you say your name, say the full name that you were given at birth.

The mantra above was from the book *"**You Are The One** by Pine G. Land. This mantra has helped me. It's all mental. It's all in the MIND. You are the creator of your own reality. The universe can be your servant when you demand it to obey your wishes. Do not obey any external entity or idea. You were created with abilities and talents. You were created to live free, in a peaceful and mentally powerful state and in love with creation.

## S69 DEATH IS JUST ONE OF MANY STOPS BEFORE REACHING DESTINATION

Death is one of the stops before reaching your destination, but on the other hand, every moment that you breathe/live, is also your current destination. Life should not be like the trip from your house to work, but a vacation trip where you enjoy every moment, away from turmoil and internal conflict.

So much mental and emotional suffering happens just by being worried or afraid to die. What's the point of living in mental and emotional chaos? Every present moment is eternal, nobody can get that away from you. Live in the moment, don't waste your life on resenting the past and/or imagining the future because you may not be happy in the moment. Meditate, practice solitude, practice deep conscious breathing so that you become centered, so that you appreciate and are grateful for the eternal moment which is the greatest gift. Do not waste away the gift. Do not be distracted by the countless poisons and distractions that  this decayed system produces.

> "We all are flawed one way or another, not by divine design but by man-made design. The flaws that we have are little viruses that have been injected in us in the form of governments, organized religions, legal documentation, feminism agenda, skin color, racism, equality, voting, lab-made so-called foods and drinks, fluoridated water and many more forms of poisons that have captured people's minds and spirits". – Pine G. Land, *You Are The One*, p,43

In the core of our true selves, we are flawless, we are eternal divine sparks/flames that can never be extinguished. This life is but a fleeting moment in this grand Cosmic design. Don't be afraid to die, be afraid to exist as if you've never lived. In the words of the great philosopher of the last century, Alan Watts,

"*When a cat falls out of a tree, it lets go itself. The cat becomes completely relaxed, and lands lightly on the ground. But if a cat were about to fall out of a tree and suddenly make up its mind that it didn't want to fall, it would become tense and rigid, and would be just a bag of broken bones upon landing. In the same way, it is the philosophy of the Tao that we are falling off a tree, at every moment of our lives. As a matter of fact, the moment we were born, we were kicked off a precipice, and we are falling, and there is nothing that can stop it. So instead of living in a state of chronic tension, and clinging to all sorts of things that are actually falling with us because the whole world is impermanent, be like a cat".*

Many people rush daily to make money or go here and there, nowhere and everywhere. For what, what is it that they want to achieve? Wealth, power? Who has ever found happiness by hoarding wealth and power? Nobody. The fact that someone never stops hoarding money or chasing something outside of themselves proves that happiness is not out there but inside, in the heart. But of course, the way the world functions, money may be needed, but you can manifest money, as long as you don't become greedy, as long as you don't end up at the point of no return. Chasing illusions creates a megalomaniac personality.

Our subconscious, which is connected with the Great Mind, used to be the main consciousness prior to the manipulation and the embellishment of ego. Our natural state is "theta state". Currently, with all the chaos in the world, for most people, the theta state is achieved automatically before going to bed and when one wakes up. Other than that, for the rest of the day, people live in a rush mode, distracted and anxious all day long; that would be "beta state".

> **"Money is just numbers and numbers never end, if it requires money to reach happiness, the search for happiness will never end"**
>
> - Bob Marley

# S70 SUBCONSCIOUSNESS-UNDENIABLE UNIVERSAL FACTS

The subconscious mind is always awake and alert, it never sleeps. When you fall asleep, the body sleeps, the subconscious mind never does. Over 90% of our lives are controlled by our subconscious mind. It is true, that whatever activities that you do daily, you do them consciously, but your actions are simply a playback of the subconscious mind. Everything gets recorded in the subconscious by repetition, the more you repeat something, the more you are entangled with whatever it is that you are interacting with (physically, mentally or emotionally).

The subconscious mind has no verbal language. The subconscious mind speaks through intuition. The more distracted you are, the less intuition will be there for you to sense. Your subconscious mind takes everything literally. It doesn't understand jokes. It can't distinguish facts from fiction, that's why it is important to speak positively about anything or else negativity will be recorded and playback through your actions.

One of the ways to communicate with your subconscious mind is through dreams. Dreams are not just dreams but messages from your subconscious mind or your higher self. Dreams are directly related to anything you think, say or do daily. It is not logical, your subconscious is the feeling mind. The feeling mind is much more powerful than the thinking mind. Through thinking, we overanalyze and we end up liking or disliking someone, holding a grudge on people, becoming jealous, envy, egomaniacs/selfish, but through the feeling mind, we feel and sense the truth automatically with the thinking mind out of the way. This system we live in is designed to keep mankind living in the mind, hence the daily chaos that has people running and chasing their own tail with no exit/solution in the horizon.

Only 5-10% of our brain is logical. By thinking in logical terms, we create unnecessary chaos in our lives. Trusting your intuition is essential in gaining knowledge and understanding without overthinking logically. This doesn't mean that we don't need conscious reasoning. This is about not operating mostly on logic. Many struggles/hate among friends or siblings happen because of the logical mind. The mind is polluted with greed and other poisons, therefore the person's intuition is suppressed.

## S71 BIRTHDAY CELEBREATION, DATES, CLOCKS & CALENDARS AGES YOU FASTER

The ancients used symbols, gestures and the stars (sky and all other luminaries) to communicate. They communicate telepathically also. The moment we began writing, is when we were nose diving in consciousness. There are four stages in the cycle of life, Golden

Age, Silver Age, Bronze Age and Iron Age. In the Golden Age we are automatically and fully connected to our true selves and the Creation, the Source of All. In the Silver age people need rituals to keep connected. In the Bronze Age people lost connection with the Prime Creator/Creation. And there is the Iron Age or "Kali Yuga" or otherwise known as the Dark Age, where mankind completely has lost connection to the Divine. We have been in "Kali Yuga" or in the Dark Age for a very long time, hence we need to write to communicate with each other. When we are fully connected to ourselves and the Divine Creation, we automatically communicate telepathically 24/7, just as easy as we breathe. Writing causes us to have a shorter life span. But because we lost connection to true knowledge, we also began abusing our bodies, especially sexual energy which further reinforced the shortening of mankind's lifespan.

Every time you celebrate a birthday, you are actually celebrating death, you are celebrating one more year taken of your finite lifespan. Life is infinite, but it becomes finite through the abuse of the body and the mind. What you believe you become. Many people calculate the years until their retirement. What this does is training the trillions of cells for self-destruction, I.E. slow death. Your DNA is designed to self-replicate/regenerate. But for that to happen, the energy or life force must not be stagnant through dead foods and drinks, sexual indulgence and anything that goes against the natural law.

All life you have been bombarded by numbers, and in the case of death, you have been bombarded by the numbers 80, 90, 70, 30, or any other number which was the age of when someone passed away. In your subconscious it is recorded (through your own beLIEf) that people die at a certain age and that that is normal. But that is only true for you if you believe that. I know this may sound crazy but try to understand that you create your own reality. Your physical body has to obey what you think or believe. Now, of course it doesn't mean that if you don't believe in aging and all of a sudden you become immortal.

What you think and feel, must reflect what you eat, drink and whether you exercise or not. It must be a whole package effort. It won't happen in one day. It took years for the human body to be polluted, but it will also take some time for it to be cleansed if one truly makes a great effort. But most people refuse to let go of their beliefs or their addictions to foods, drinks, pornography, alcohol, dead flesh etc.

Many times people are shocked or sad when someone they knew died on the day of their birthday or 5 days before their birthday or 1 day before Christmas etc. First of all, every day is equally important to enjoy life. Secondly, why should it matter what the day is? Do you think the dead care what day it was? No, these are the living ones who are stuck in traditions, dates and calendars.

## S72 CREMATE, DON'T BURY THOSE WHO CHANGE FORM

If you are pregnant, or even if you have little children do not take them to a funeral or the cemetery. Unhealed spirits that haven't yet let go of this realm, linger around in cemeteries, funerals or hospitals and they can affect innocent children. Not only that, but even if you were to have sexual intercourse on the day/night of the death situation for the purpose to conceive the child, one of those spirits could reincarnate as your child. When you conceive a child, both future parents' physical, emotional, mental and spiritual state must be of high vibrational frequency.

Personally, I would recommend one to be cremated as opposed to buried. Being buried might cause the spirit to linger at the cemetery as opposed to moving on in their journey. But when one is cremated, there is no fixed space in the physical world for the spirit to linger around. The lingering around happens for many reasons but another reason is the unfinished work someone had before passing away and/or disagreement they had with their family members, friends etc. It is very important not to be tied to any person. Loving someone is good as long as the love is not tied with strings like a puppet. It must be unconditional. If it is, then when one passes away, they cannot be attached to you anymore.

In my will (*if I pass away), I wrote that I wish to be cremated. The main reason for this is not to waste or pollute a piece of land and also I do not want my children to visit their *ex-father at the cemetery which is full of lingering spirits. I do not want the tomb to make them cry, I want them to remember the happy/laughing moments.

*if I pass away – We are eternal, not just spiritually but also on a physical level. If people practiced 100% natural raw food diet, and all other steps until they became breatharians, plus full continence/chastity, there would be no reason why someone should age or die. This seems impossible because we have been brainwashed for many generations. It takes about two months for an information to be repeated before it becomes permanent in the subconscious of a human. For how long have we seen that people die? All life, and not just for 2 months. Never underestimate the power of the subconscious mind.

*ex-father – Most, if not all people, refer to their deceased parents (children, friends etc.) as if they're still their parents. That is a lie. The truth is not concerned with what we feel, believe or think. Everyone has a role to play, when they're done with the role, meaning when they pass away, they will reincarnate as another person, somewhere else, at a different time. They are not your parents anymore. Disagree all you want, my intention is for you to realize that attachment to people keeps you enslaved in a 3D reality, a reality of suffering. Anything in this realm that you are too attached to, will be what will deceive you when you have to choose between moving on to higher realms of existence or whether you will be magnetized and be reincarnated again in the underworld, the realm of wars, famine, struggling, killing, drugs etc.

Everyone you meet in life, whether they are good or evil people, they are temporary. Everyone is a test subject. Guess what happens if you fail a test, you will keep repeating the same exam over and over again until you pass. In the context of life and death, if you don't pass, you will keep reincarnating over and over again until you get it right.

Another way for a low vibration (unhealed/confused) spirit to enter your auric field (consciousness/unconsciousness) is when you have a sexual climax/orgasm. When you have an orgasm, for a few seconds you lose your consciousness, which means that that's when you become a portal for entities from the astral realm to travel onto this one through you. Many people would disagree with this, for two reasons:

1) - Pleasure. The feeling of orgasm is so good and powerful that makes a person lose rationality.

2) – Fake studies. Sex/porn is the spiritual weapon number one used to control humanity. A lot of people read studies about the benefits of orgasm. There is zero benefit from orgasms. You may feel temporarily good, but the consequences are detrimental to the body, mind and spirit. Every time you orgasm, you waste seminal fluid, which is the building block of intelligence. Seminal fluid contains phosphorus,

the most important nourishment for the brain.

The definition of insanity is to keep repeating the same thing over and over and expecting different results. If you realize that there is something wrong in the world or in your life, then perhaps you should do something different as opposed to doing the same things you've been doing for a long time. What do many people that eat ice cream do when their throat feels frozen, they keep eating it. What do people that feel bloated from food do, they continue consuming food that makes them feel bloated every time.

Here's another way a spirit can possess you. Online there are many people who say something similar:

*"I'm feeling drawn to you. I'm sensing something important for you that you need to know. I have a message from your ancestors, give me your left palm etc."*

First of all, you are your own ancestors. Everything from the past that is for your higher purpose, is embedded in your DNA, in your cells. Some of these people have genuine intention, it is their business, they need to survive just like anyone else, but many of these are affected by negative spirits from the astral realm. Many others are scams. When you give permission for your energy to be accessed by someone else, it is like giving the key to your castle, the key to your DNA. Be careful on this subject. Realize that you are both the key and the castle.

## S73 RIGHTEOUS PATH NEEDS EFFORT AND DISCIPLINE

Celibacy if you are alone, or tantric sex if you decide to share your life with the opposite gender.
No fluoride as it will diminish your pineal gland's light.
Fasting will make sure that your internal organs become organs of intuition and not a sewage system.
Meditation pulls you away from the conscious materialistic mind.
Yoga, Taichi, Chi gong (exercise/training in general) allows the energy in the body to freely flow and supply the nervous system and consciousness.
Engaging in sun gazing or sunbathing can nourish cells with cosmic rays, reducing or eliminating the need for food when practiced correctly.

Fruit (avoid seedless fruit), vegetables, herbs, seed and nuts; the 1<sup>st</sup> major step in becoming healthy, until you are ready for more steps (as you already read the other steps in PART 1).

The 1<sup>st</sup> step to begin the spiritual journey is to not have sex, no masturbation, no orgasms and no arousal either. Sexual creative or destructive energy is what enslaves or frees humanity. Retain your seed/semen and ovum. The same applies to women. The equivalent 'semen retention" for women is to retain their blood and eggs. (Check the book I mentioned about how to stop menstruating and menopause, parthenogenesis etc. by Dr. Raymond W. Bernard).

The number one requirement for the awakening and the raising of your Kundalini is to retain your seed – Semen for men and blood/ eggs for women. I'm pretty sure that many would disagree with the requirement above. Some people have realized that the government is not our friend, and this makes them think they have awakened and they think their kundalini is raised, meanwhile they consume toxic foods and drinks daily, they waste their creative sexual energy/ life force by abusing their sexual glands continually. Kundalini won't rise if lifeforce is low and the body and mind are polluted. There is a difference between awakened, raised and fully raised Kundalini.

Being attracted to the opposite gender does not make you a strong person. Being a heterosexual is the most basic thing to be. You must honor the role of your gender. Considering yourself being strong; just because you are attracted to the opposite gender, is like thinking you are intelligent because you know that two + two = four.

A family foundation can only be strong only when both the man and the woman honor their natural roles which are: Men must be the protectors and women must be the nurturers. A lot of men boast/ show off to their friends or society being strong but when they have to face their partners they are weak. Being strong physically is a must when it's about protecting the women but not to use your physical strength against them.

The strength of a man toward his wife/girlfriend are his thoughts and emotions. The muscles are worthless if you can't handle your thoughts and emotions. Many women have ended up prostituting themselves in the streets or online by deceiving many men for personal gain. If men practiced semen retention they would become strong therefore there would be many strong men for all those women that had no choice but to stray off their path as a result of men becoming weak. This is not about blaming women or men for their choices. The poison in women's and men's minds was injected by others that have no interest in happiness among people/ couples. You can refuse the poisons (porn, ejaculating, alcohol, lying, deceiving, materialism etc.).

## S74 6 THIEVES, 7 EMOTIONS & 7 INJURIES, 10 WEAKNESSES

The human mind doesn't have any innate tendencies toward staying/being still. The spirit dwells in the mind (mind and brain are not the same thing), because of this, when the spirit is in control, the mind can be still, especially through meditation. When you train yourself to meditate daily and become a self-aware person even when you do not have your eye closed through meditation, then your daily life becomes the meditation. The human mind (not the brain) does not have tendencies toward activities, but because knowledge dwells in the mind (processed by the brain), then the mind becomes active when knowledge is in charge.

There are six residues in the human body. The six impulses produce six ducts. Six thieves emerge from these ducts. Because of the six thieves, the six spirits fade away. When the six spirits wither, the human body falls into the six existences. What are the six thieves?

In *Cultivating Stillness*, the Taoist Manual for Transforming Body and Mind, by Eva Wong, talks about the thieves, the emotions, the injuries and the weaknesses.

The **S I X THIEVES** – The **eyes**, **ears**, **nose**, **tongue**, **body** and **mind**. We are exposed daily to a range of stimuli, including images, shapes, foods, drinks, information, fragrances, and sounds of varying frequencies. These steal our time, our joy, or existence. The mind needs to be still if it wants to communicate with the Great Spirit. Since youthful age, children are taught to lie, deceive, consume poisons etc. When they become adults, they are already part of the herd mentality. Teach children to appreciate the little things, to be content with little. I do not mean to teach them to be poor. We are all rich when we manifest from a place of love. Just teach them to not be greedy, or else they might end up in a place of no return.

It is easier to teach a child or an adult that knows nothing, rather than teaching ourselves. Someone with a lot of knowledge (mostly bad), will have to first undo/throw away the poison they learned since they were children. Most people create the belief that what they know is the truth, and that is a lie, for most people. We know nothing – and this is the beginning of wisdom. Pay attention to what information you absorb from the internet, Tv, friends etc. Pay attention to what you eat, drink, smell. Pay attention to the words you speak. Your tongue is soft, but strong enough to hurt someone, directly or indirectly.

## The S E V E N EMOTIONS & S E V E N INJURIES

Are emotions good to have or not? Without emotions we would be like walking dead robots. Too much emotional excitement is equally harmful as not having any emotions at all. **Happiness, sadness, anger, cruelty, love, desire** and **fear** are the seven emotions. Three out of the seven emotions seem innocent; those three are, love, desire and happiness. A lot of people strive or look for happiness, through desires which in turn would make them feel loved or in love. They are all illusions. No matter how we analyze the emotions, they will harm us or others in one way or another if we do not realize that stillness and being in the moment would bring us love, anything we desire and happiness, but only if we appreciate life and everything in it for what they are, in the grand scheme of things, including appreciating and being grateful for the little things.

*Excessive sadness harms the lungs*
*Excessive love harms the spirit*
*Excessive fear harms the gall-bladder*
*Excessive happiness harms the heart*
*Excessive anger harms the liver*
*Excessive desire harms the spleen*
*Excessive cruelty harms sensitivity*

The above seven can easily be misunderstood or be rejected by many because many people are, in one way or another lured in the trap of being distracted by all sorts of foods, drinks, agendas, and information which pollutes the mind; which in turn creates emotional chaos. When you live in the moment, you don't have expectations, and if you don't have expectations, you will not be emotionally unstable, because supposed scenarios that supposedly could happen in the supposed future, don't exist in your reality. How many times do we become extremely emotional when we think about some negative/positive experiences from the past or stories we make up in our mind about the future?

## The T E N  WEAKNESSES

Do humans have weaknesses? Of course they do, not by default though. We become weak for all sorts of reasons which are initiated in the mind. Without the mind, the body wouldn't even be able to move.

*If you stand too much, your bones will weaken*
*If you sit too much, the blood will weaken*
*If you walk too much your tendons will weaken*
*If you sleep too much, your meridians will weaken*
*If you see too much, your spirit will weaken*
*If you think too much, your spleen will weaken*
*If you listen too much, your generative force will weaken*
*If you eat too much, your heart will weaken*
*If you speak too much, your vital energy will weaken*
*If you have too much sex, your generative energy will dissipate*

Society is bombarded with toxicity from all angles, in all forms. All the toxicity in the foods, drinks, technological devices etc., harm all the parts of the body, some more and some less. These poisons create havoc in one's being, which manifest as diseases, visual ones or not. Majority of diseases are non-physical but mental.

That's why meditation is good because you don't listen or see or speak things that would create emotional chaos in you. Fasting is good because you would not eat to the point that your heart would weaken. Exercise is good so that your blood won't weaken. You get the point. Minimize sleeping, seeing, standing, sitting, walking (assuming you walk in the extreme), thinking, listening, eating, speaking and sexing.

Cultivate your original existence with calmness and self-awareness, otherwise your spirit will depart. The spirit departs when the body and mind wither. Blood is the river of life. A polluted or disturbed blood will cause the spirit to loosen up from the physical body. A loosened up body is unstable and the spirit will leave, little by little until it is the final moment when one has no choice but to pass and then reincarnation is guaranteed. Cultivate stillness in the mind, health in the body and light/divinity in the spirit.

*The Confucian sages say:*
**"See not that which you abstain from;**
**hear not that which stirs up your fears"**

Eva Wong, in *Cultivating Stillness*, has this to say: "*The Buddhists Teach that there should be no thoughts in the eyes, ears, nose, tongue, and body; no color, no sound, no fragrance, no taste, and no touch. The Taoists say that forms are illusive. The three religions teach the same principles. Act according to the three teachings and you will be free of cravings*".

In the above quote, you read the word "religion". In its most core, in the beginning, all religions were created to guide humanity. Many people dismiss or ridicule religion because they have been conditioned to think religion as a bad thing. And they are right, but because there is a difference between religion and organized religion. Many dismiss religion, many others blindly believe religion (the organized one), and the truth is lost and gone with the wind. A lot of truths are hidden in all the religions, the major and many other smaller ones. Religions were created because mankind had fallen from grace. Rules or guidelines were needed to control them.

Those who possess self-control do not require external control. Only he who is confused, lost and unconscious, needs a master or better a parent. Look at humanity, they are still lost, even though many have awakened in these last two decades. There is nobody to come and save you, you are your own savior. If you carefully decipher the message that all religions want people to know is that you are your own savior. Until people realize this, they will continue to worship external deities, public figures, politicians, actors, singers, materialism etc., and they will continue to chase their own tail with no sight to salvation, their soul will be chained (metaphorically).

Yin and yang (or yin-yang) is a complex relational concept in Chinese philosophy that has developed over thousands of years. Briefly put, the meaning of yin and yang is that the universe is governed by a cosmic duality, sets of two opposing and complementing principles or cosmic energies that can be observed in nature such as:

**Y I N** – Male, logical, active, the Sun, hot, energy, the day, the mountain, superficial, aware, discovered, expiration, the fire.

**Y A N G** – Female, intuitive, passive, the Moon, cold, matter, Unconscious, Hidden, the water, inspiration, the river, the night.

What is the yin/yang symbol and why is it designed and depicted like the image on the right for thousands of years?

The yin-yang symbol (also known as the Tai Chi symbol) consists of a circle divided into two halves by a curved line. One half of the circle is black, typically representing the yin side; the other is white, for the yang side. A dot of each color is situated near the center of the other's half. The two halves are thus intertwining across a spiral-like curve that splits the whole into semicircles, and the small dots represent the idea that both sides carry the seed of the other.

The white dot in the black area and the black dot in the white area connote coexistence and unity of opposites to form a whole. The curvy line signifies that there are no absolute separations between the two opposites. The yin-yang symbol, then, embodies both sides: duality, paradox, unity in diversity, change, and harmony.

To be healthy, one must balance both yin and yang. In today's world, the majority of people are confused and not healthy because the yin and yang energies in them are over powering them. Many men have been emasculated (overpowered by their own feminine/yin energy) and many women have become masculinized, they are overpowered by their own masculine/yang energy. Whether you are a woman or a man, you are both energies in one. You will never see total balance in you if you are predominant in the opposite energy of your biological sex.

## S75 CHEWING GUM - A VERY HARMFUL POISON

Chewing gum tricks your body into thinking that you are eating, therefore, your stomach will release the powerful digestive fluid which is needed to break down and digest the food. But the stomach is empty. What this does is, damages the lining of the stomach. Over time, holes may be created on the stomach walls and you may need surgery or take pills for the rest of your life like some people I know who to this day take medications. But everything is fixable naturally. Those people believe that only pills can heal them. The pills simply keep us like walking dead zombies.

Why do people chew gum? Because of nutrients/vitamins?

Absolutely NOT. People chew gum when they are bored, anxious and to be cool. Your health is more important. Chewing gum when you are anxious, it may relax and calm you down just like a smoker when they light a cigarette, but the damage to the body is detrimental. Temporary relief is not worth it to pay with your life in the long run.

## S76 BE REBORN LIKE PINOCCHIO

Pinocchio is a wooden boy and he constantly tells lies. This is a metaphor for us humans that lie to ourselves and others on a daily basis. We have to be reborn and walk the path of truth from being paralyzed from beliefs and ignorance to thinking for ourselves and being truthful, by connecting with our inner selves and the creation/nature. When they hear about the word/name 'Pinocchio', most people think of it as the wooden boy that lies and that's it. They simply remember the cartoon or the animated movie. But every movie exists for at least two specific reasons, to distract/entertain people that are too tired to think for themselves and for those who seek to know and as the famous quote says, *"Seek and you shall find"*. Pinocchio means pineal gland. Pin(e) and Occhio (in Italian which derives from Latin) which means eye, which is the third eye. The pineal gland is physical, but the third eye is non-physical/astral. Just as we have a physical brain, and a non-physical mind.

## S77 MOVIES - THEY ARE BOTH THE POISON & THE REMEDY

Movies are for two kinds of people, those who want to be entertained/distracted or those who seek to find. In many movies there are killings, but it doesn't mean that you will be inclined to kill. The real reason for the propaganda is for the viewers to become desensitized to life. When wars happen, people still continue with their self-destructive habits, because they have been desensitized. The subconscious mind sees everything as fact, including movies, so when wars or killings happen, people don't rise up for the injustice happening. People only voice their concern when something happens to them personally. The propaganda applies the same about the news channels, magazines, TV shows, conversation with people, in social media etc.

Someone who drinks alcohol or smokes cigarettes, when they watch these poisons being flashed in the movies, they will be inclined to consume these products, even if at the moment they weren't feeling like drinking or smoking. Other people would be more aware and careful to not consume these products. When you watch erotic movies, porn or sexualization in general, you may get aroused and make a mistake having sex with the wrong person and at the wrong time. What do I mean by "*the wrong time*"? If your girlfriend or wife is pregnant, you should not have any sexual intercourse or anything sexual at all. In this book, you read the consequences of having sexual intercourse while the woman is in gestation period.

If movies were about loving one another, being connected to nature and ourselves, finding our purpose etc., then there would be no movies made. Movies exist because slavery, distraction, struggling, purposelessness and ignorance exist.

## S78 THE TRUTH ABOUT THE TRUTH

People don't want to hear the truth. They want to hear what they already believe is the truth, even if it is not the truth. That is the truth about the truth. We are a demoralized society. Our nervous system is fractured, the mind is overloaded and the physical body is pumped with toxins daily. How could a society want to hear the truth when it is damaged to the core? The solution is within us all. Instead of adding more in our mind, we should take things off, one at a time, anything that doesn't serve us anymore.

We are mirrors of each other. Any inanimate object must not be seen as a living thing, or else it will steal you away from purifying your soul. You are not who you think you are when you see yourself in the mirror.

> "The mirror is a worthless invention. The only way to truly see yourself is in the reflection of someone else's eyes" – *Love Satya*

This Archontic system thrives on human's suffering and deaths. Any next life should be better than the previous one and not worse. As if the previous lifetimes' trauma wasn't enough, the parasites that manage this satanic parasitic system inflict even more trauma when they cut the umbilical cord of the baby, where the baby receives less blood, oxygen and stem cells from the mother, less nutrients, creation codes, protection etc.

The ultimate goal is to not have to reincarnate anymore. We are created to not age, nor die. The majority of people would laugh at the idea that a human is created to not die. They would laugh because the conditioning is very deep, just as I was laughing years ago, about a lot of things that we now know to be true. That something makes sense, it doesn't mean that it is true. Just as if something doesn't make sense, it doesn't mean it is false either. What is true and what is untrue is in direct proportion to the current knowledge and understanding we have of ourselves and the world.

Bruce Lee said: *"You don't need coffee; you need rest. You don't need to shout; you need to express yourself clearly. You don't need to demean; you need to cultivate your art. Life is not about external stimuli, but about nurturing the spirit with what truly matters: walking, laughing, creating, reading, and feeling. True strength lies in finding inner peace, in balancing the internal with the external. Do what you believe, and deeply believe in what you do"*.

Your truth is not my truth and vice versa. What is true now, may not be true tomorrow, next week or the next year. There are truths that apply daily which are based on spiritual growth; the truth changes form according to our level of knowledge and understanding, but there are also ultimate/divine truths (look into the *Hermetic Principles/Natural Laws*) which apply to everyone, everywhere at all times.

## S79 IGNORANCE IS A CHOICE

In the universe, cycles govern everything, including the rise and fall of consciousness, consequently the rise and fall of civilizations. The Great Cycle or the Cosmic cycle presents an approximately 26,000 year cycle divided in 2,100-2,200 year intervals for each of the twelve zodiac ages. In the Age of Aquarius, a new path unfolds, balance and harmony is returning, which means higher consciousness is also returning. Chaos and ignorance happens only through lower consciousness. Those who refuse to rise in consciousness will be doomed. Creation doesn't reward or punish; we punish ourselves through our daily choices. No matter the age you are, you have the capability to rise, and definitely do not neglect children, teach them love and care, self-awareness, detachment and to walk the spiritual path of self-mastery.

If a dog attacks a kitten, the kitten's mother will attack the dog and protect his child. The cat will not care about prison/man-made laws. You have the universal right to protect your children even if you have to take someone's life away for wanting to kill your child. In our modern society many parents willingly give away their children to be slaughtered (metaphorically speaking) through bad foods and drinks, vaccinations, entertainment etc. People have lost connection with nature. Your life can improve just by observing the animals. Ignorance doesn't get us anywhere.

## S80 THIRTYTHREE, THE NUMBER WHICH OFFERS FREEDOM

The 33 segments of the Spinal Column are called JACOB'S LADDER in the Bible. When Jacob climbs to the top, he is filled with God and names the place Peniel. The 33 steps correspond with the 33 columns of the human spine. Hanukkah the OIL of CHRIST is a spinal fluid which rises up through the spinal column as the Kundalini energy rises up through the 7 chakras and can reach the Pineal Gland/The Spiritual Third Eye.

When the oil reach The Place Of Skull = Golgotha, then it is crucified (to crucify means to increase in power) it remains three days and a half, ((the moon's period (tropical and sidereal days) in a sign)) in the tomb (cere-bellum) and on the third day ascends to the Pineal Gland that connects the cerebellum with the Optic Thalamus, the Central Eye in the Throne of God that is the chamber overtopped by the hollow (hallowed) caused by the curve of the cerebrum (the "Most High" of the body) which is the "Temple of the Living God" and then the person achieves higher consciousness and becomes enlightenment.

The number 33 is very significant and holds a very deep esoteric; hidden meaning. Jesus was crucified at the age of 33, in 33 A.D. Jesus also performed 33 written miracles, 33 is also the number at which water boils according to the Newton scale, the Vedic Religion has 33 deities, 33 is the degree at which all points of the universe collide, The divine name Elohim appears 33 times in the opening chapter of the Genesis creation story, Islamic prayer beads are usually arranged in sets of 33, the numerical representation of the Star of David is 33, as well as Amen. In numerology 33 is a master number. - Carina Alva

The ancients, through the Bible, other sacred texts and artworks have always told us the truth, but only those who were seeking it, found it. Nowadays, we have the truth right in front of our eyes, and yet, many of us refuse to believe it or to do something about it. Doing something about it, means to work on ourselves. Anything toxic we eat, drink, say or think, contributes to the pollution of the sacred secretion which is produced once a month in the brain. One other thing which prohibits the sacred secretion to carry up the spine the Kundalini energy, is sexual incontinence for both men and women. The DNA symbol, or the Caduceus is represented by the staff and the two serpents, this is a symbol used by the ancient masters and Gnostics. Even if you ate and drank pure food and drinks, the Kundalini will awaken but it will never be raised fully if you waste your lunar/solar atoms through ejaculation, menstruation, orgasms and masturbations. We are created to perfection; we cannot cheat the great divine design; we cannot skip grades.

Your consciousness resides in the brain, Jesus' death at the age of 33 symbolizes the Kundalini energy rising up the spinal vertebrae all the way to your pineal gland, where the seat of consciousness is. That's what Jesus' story was about, escaping the dense physical body and reaching Creation, the Void, the Center of All, or the true Garden of Eden. Understand the bigger picture, instead of arguing with others about the real name of Jesus, or if he existed or not, or if his story is the only story of that caliber or if it was copied from earlier ancient texts. Don't get caught in semantics. Become an observer, so that you see the bigger picture.

Become an eagle where you see beyond the horizon, where you see reality for what it is. The 6th chakra (third eye) symbol has two petals but also they resemble wings, to symbolize the eagle/flying because when your third eye is opened, you feel like you are flying, where nothing weighs you down.

THE TREASURE HAS BEEN
WITHIN US ALL SINCE BIRTH

# Bibliography, plus more sources to further your knowledge

*To Be Reborn* by Tamo A. Replica
*The Internal Dragon: The Art of Self-Mastery* by J.J.
*You Are Not A Strawman You Are The Zygote* by Saimir X. Kercanaj
*Battles Between Shadow and Light* by Wes Penre
*Blue Blood, True Blood* by Stewart A. Swerdlow
*Self-Empowerment* by Saimir Kercanaj
*Natural Treasure: Quest For Knowledge, Health and Freedom* by Blake Cyrier
*Gain Wisdom Through Practiced Knowledge* by Rimias K. Neo
*You Are The One* by Pine G. Land
*Body Mind Soul: As You Believe So Shall It Be by* Saimir Kercanaj
*Cultivating Stillness* by Ewa Wong
*Creation of the Superman* by Dr. Raymond W. Bernard, with commentary by Liquid Metal
*I Am The Key That Opens All Doors* by Saimir Kercanaj
*Food of the Gods* by Terence McKenna
*The Phoenix Protocol* by August Dunning
*Juice Fasting & Detoxification* by Steve Meyerowitz
*Man's Higher Consciousness* by Hilton Hotema
*Brain Gain* by Danavir Goswami

https://www.thoughtco.com/yin-and-yang-629214
https://breakingnewsenglish.com/1504/150416-high-heels-300.htm
https://www.rd.com/article/how-to-meditate/
https://www.yogabasics.com/practice/pranayama/diaphragmatic-breathing-in-yoga/
https://www.metabolomicclinic.com/english/telomere_analysis-na-192.html

# NOTES

NOTES

# NOTES

# NOTES

Printed in Dunstable, United Kingdom

63544711R10109